IN TWO CHINAS

BY K. M. PANIKKAR

Asia and Western Dominance
The Founding of the Kashmir State
India and the Indian Ocean

K. M. PANIKKAR

In Two Chinas

Memoirs
of a Diplomat

☆

LONDON
GEORGE ALLEN & UNWIN LTD
RUSKIN HOUSE   MUSEUM STREET

FIRST PUBLISHED IN 1955

PRINTED IN GREAT BRITAIN
in 12 *point Bembo type*
BY UNWIN BROTHERS LTD
WOKING AND LONDON

FOREWORD

No attempt is made in the present volume to give a connected history of the period between 1948 and 1952 when I was in China successively as Ambassador of India to the National Government at Nanking and later to the People's Republic of China in Peking. It is no more than a record of personal experiences and impressions during what was undoubtedly a most critical period of Chinese history. The final stages in the break-down of the Kuomintang regime took place, so to say, before my very eyes. It was also given to me to witness the rise of the new Chinese State. More significantly, it fell to me to be associated with all the negotiations relating to the Korean war during the first difficult days preceding the Chinese intervention in Korea and the discussions for a cease-fire, which, though abortive at the time, laid the foundations for the agreement negotiated two years later.

I need not add specifically that the views expressed in the book are entirely personal and should not in any way be considered as reflecting the opinions of the Government of India.

I have also to acknowledge with gratitude the assistance I have received from Mr. Shiv Shastri and Mr. R. C. Asthana in the difficult but necessary task of proof-reading. I am also grateful to Mr. Geoffrey Hudson, Fellow of St. Anthony's College, Oxford, for helping me with the proper spelling of Chinese names.

LONDON,   K. M. PANIKKAR
March 21, 1955.

CONTENTS

CHAPTER I

INDIA'S AMBASSADOR
TO CHINA

I HAD been told by Sarojini Naidu a few months before the declaration of independence that Prime Minister Nehru had decided to post me abroad as ambassador as soon as the work of securing the accession of the princely states to the Union of India was completed. The main brunt of that work which was to create a united India out of the patchwork of provinces and princely states had fallen on Krishnamachari and myself. With the active support of Lord Mountbatten, then not only Governor-General but also the representative of the Crown in its relations with Indian Rulers, we were able by negotiations with national leaders to fill the vacuum created by the abolition of the paramountcy of the British Crown over these states and bring about their peaceful accession before the 15th of August, 1947, the date fixed for the termination of British authority in India.

A few days before the 15th of August, I had been invited to join the Indian delegation to the General Assembly of the United Nations which was to meet in New York by the middle of September. As this was the first international conference at which independent India was being represented, I was particularly happy that the Prime Minister had selected me to join the delegation which was to be led by Mrs. Vijayalakshmi Pandit. The Maharaja of Bikaner willingly agreed to my deputation. But unexpected difficulties arose at the last moment. The partition of India had led to an upheaval which no one had anticipated. The unfortunate province of the Punjab was up in flames. Muslims in the border areas of the Indian Union and Hindus and Sikhs in West Pakistan suddenly found themselves forcibly uprooted and driven away from their homes. The inhuman cruelty, deliberate massacres and large-scale relapse into atavistic barbarism which were displayed on

both sides are only painful memories now. But they shocked the
world at the time. The State of Bikaner of which I was the Prime
Minister was situated in the very centre of these troubles. To the
north and east of it lay East Punjab where Hindus and Sikhs had
joined hands against the Muslims and were indulging in murder,
loot and arson. To the west of it lay Bahawalpur in Pakistan, where
on one single day five thousand Hindus had been massacred. From
all over Pakistan, Hindu and Sikh refugees were pouring into the
State. The Muslim population in Bikaner itself was in a state of
panic. I was well aware that if I did not stop the conflagration on
the borders of Bikaner and prevent it from spreading, it could not
be stopped and would reach as far as Bombay with consequences
which no one could foresee. The demand in Bikaner for expelling
the Muslims to Pakistan was mounting. In the irrigated part of the
State, known as Ganga Nagar, there was a powerful Sikh
community, and in view of what their brethren in the Punjab had
suffered they were thirsting for the blood of the Muslims. To add
to my troubles, many thousands of refugees from the neighbouring
State of Bahawalpur in Pakistan had also entered that area and added
fuel to the fire.

I was determined at all costs to prevent the trouble spreading
into Bikaner, not merely because of humanitarian considerations,
but because I was well aware of the consequences of arousing the
dormant anti-Muslim feeling of the Rajputs, and I knew that if
there was the least weakening on my part Rajputana would
repeat, perhaps in an exaggerated form, the terrible history of the
Punjab. The Maharaja, Sadul Singh, fully supported me in this
view, and when the first news arrived of troubles in the Punjab,
with the Maharaja's permission I sent the best part of the State
Army to the Ganga Canal area on the Punjab and Bahawalpur
frontier. I toured the area personally and made it clear that the State
would not tolerate any attack on its Muslim subjects, that the army
had orders to shoot rioters, and that the civil authorities were
empowered to impose collective fines and confiscate land. Within
a week the situation had become so quiet that I thought I would be
able with a clear conscience to join the delegation and go to New
York.

But in the first week of September a new and more frightening situation arose. Though the State was unusually calm and there had not been a single incident, news reached me that on different spots on the border thousands of Muslim refugees were collecting in camps with the intention of marching through Bikaner to Pakistan. These refugees, totalling 80,000 in three camps, were threatening to cross into Bikaner territory. The military guards provided by the Government of India for these camps were altogether inadequate as the bulk of the Indian Army was still in Pakistan and the available forces in India were required for more important work. Bands of organized hooligans bent on attacking the refugee camps were known to be in the vicinity and it was obvious to me that, if large-scale trouble broke out between them, the refugees would forcibly enter the State at different points and cause confusion. I tried my best to persuade the Government of India to provide trains for evacuating these menacing groups. I undertook even to put railway wagons at their disposal if the Government could find military guards for the trains. Harried and harassed by the problem of a few million Hindu and Sikh refugees uprooted and driven out of their homes in the Punjab, the Government of India was in no position to help me. Seeing how matters stood and how every hour the situation was becoming more dangerous at different points on the frontier, I took, on my own responsibility, a very risky decision. I decided to offer to escort the refugees across the State, partly by special trains over the Bikaner State Railway and partly on foot across the sands of Bikaner. It was a difficult decision to take, as public opinion in the State was greatly inflamed and in the Ganga Nagar area through which they had to pass there were many thousand refugees from Pakistan all crying for vengeance. When I explained the position to the Maharaja, he agreed enthusiastically and made it widely known that any interference with the passenger trains carrying Muslims to Pakistan, either by the people of the State or by the refugees, would meet with his stern displeasure. The first convoy went across to Pakistan safely without a single incident. Taking courage, I then ordered a second convoy, this time on foot, with only police escort, to march across the State. The organization necessary for marching a few thousand people, including women and children, over 200 miles in sand was very considerable. Food and water had to be provided; the local population had to be kept away, and precautions had at all times to be taken that there was no surprise attack by angry Hindu refugees. When this weary procession also reached Pakistan I heaved a sigh of relief. The Maharaja was also extremely happy. He felt pride in the fact that his was the only State where not only no anti-Muslim incidents had taken place, but where conditions were so normal that thousands of Muslim refugees could be convoyed across with only a police escort. He felt that the situation was normal and that I could now safely go to New York to take part in the work of the General Assembly.

The strain of the last few weeks had been terrible and I was myself satisfied after a tour of the State that nothing serious was likely to happen. So I left Bikaner on the 17th of September for New York, breaking the journey in London for two days in order to discuss matters with Krishna Menon and other friends. When I reached New York, the Assembly had already been in session for a week, and my place in the delegation had been temporarily filled by Bidhan Chandra Roy, later Chief Minister of Bengal, who then happened to be in New York.

The delegation consisted of Mrs. Vijayalakshmi Pandit, leader, Raja Maharaj Singh (later Governor of Bombay), Mr. Fazl Ali, Chief Justice of the Patna High Court, Mr. Setalwad, Advocate-General of India, B. Shiva Rao, and myself, with a group of distinguished alternates and advisers. From the beginning Mrs. Pandit showed her trust in me, for on the very day of my arrival she asked me to accompany her to a conversation with Manuelsky, the veteran Bolshevik who was the leader of the Ukranian delegation to the General Assembly. We motored down from Lake Success to an immense and palatial establishment some miles away. After an elaborate lunch we settled down to a talk. Mrs. Pandit had asked of him the reason for the less cordial attitude of the Soviet Union to the Indian delegation this year. Manuelsky was frank. "What is your interest in Korea and Greece? To us these are vital areas for our defence. Why should India interest herself against our interest in these matters?"—such was the general line of his argument. It was clear that Russia had become uncertain of India's attitude and was generally suspicious of our approach to questions of vital interest to her.

The 1947 session of the General Assembly constituted in many ways the great dividing line. It was the first meeting after the Marshall Plan had been put into effect. It was the last meeting before the changes in Czechoslovakia, which transformed that country into a People's Democracy within the framework of Soviet defence. The East-West rivalry was in process of becoming crystallized and the Soviet *bloc* was making a serious effort to show the world that America and the Western Allies were moving away definitely from the wartime agreements which in their opinion constituted the bases of the United Nations. The Korean and the Greek issues provided them with ammunition for their attack. The Soviet position in regard to Korea was a simple one. Its attitude was that the General Assembly by its charter was incompetent to discuss issues relating to war settlement; that Korea was one of the subjects which was reserved for settlement by discussion between the four great powers in the East, U.S.A., Britain, Soviet Union and China; and that the Assembly was usurping powers by bringing the case of Korea on its agenda. In regard to Greece, Manuelsky took the view that the problem was one of Anglo-American intervention in the internal politics of that country and that the Soviets wanted nothing more than a settlement of the Greek issue by the Greeks themselves. Manuelsky did not ask for support to the Soviet point of view, but merely neutrality.

The proceedings in the Third Committee (Economic and Social) interested me greatly, but I was more interested in the high political drama that was slowly unfolding itself. As days passed and the debates became more and more violent, degenerating often into vile abuse, it became clear that we were entering a period of prolonged international tension, in which the world was being organized into two rival camps. The motivation of Soviet action seemed to be the belief that the United States was determined to limit the expansion of communism, if necessary by a "preventive" war: that the Korean and Greek problems were the opening

moves in the great game of containing the communist state. The
U.S.A. was being shaken out of its indecision by the events in
Czechoslovakia which appeared to the western powers as a threat
to European security. I had known Jan Masaryk, the Czech
Foreign Minister, before the war when he was representing his
country in London. He was leading the Czech delegation to the
General Assembly and I found an opportunity of discussing the
issues with him. Masaryk appeared to me to be in an extremely
unhappy position. He defended vigorously the action of his
country in lining up with the Soviets and gave as his reason the
possibility of German revival with American support. The fear of
Germany seemed to haunt him. This seemed all the more strange
to me, for when I knew him in 1935–36 his friends and associates
in London were mainly German businessmen. But that of course
was before Hitler's aggression against Czechoslovakia, and the
eight years of misery that followed Hacha's visit to the Fuhrer.
Masaryk himself was a westerner in every sense.

There was another issue before the United Nations in which I
was deeply interested, and that was the Zionist claim for the
partition of Palestine and the establishment of an independent
Jewish State. I had been introduced to the great Jewish leader,
President Chaim Weizmann, as early as 1926 by Colonel Josiah
Wedgewood. I had met him again in New York in 1943, when
John Foster took me with him for an hour's conversation. With
some of the other Jewish leaders, like Ehilu Ebstein (now Elatt) and
Moshe Sharett, I had been on friendly terms for many years. On
the question of a Jewish State in Palestine, however, my sympathies were not all with the Zionists. The Indian attitude had
always been friendly to the Arabs. While sympathizing with the
claim of the Jews for a national home in Palestine, I thought that
their demand for a State based on religious exclusivism was in the
first instance likely to revive Islamic fanaticism, and secondly was
unjust to the Palestine Arabs. We on the Indian delegation were
therefore in favour of a cantonal federation in which the Jews and
Arabs would live together as neighbours. Dr. Weizmann was
living in the Savoy Plaza Hotel in New York, and with Mrs.
Pandit's approval I saw him a number of times to explain the

Indian point of view to him. He was of course very patient with me but, like all great men, adamant when it came to what he considered to be a cause of absolute justice. Weizmann was undoubtedly one of the most remarkable men I met. I felt in his presence the kind of reverence and humility which I used to feel in the presence of Mahatma Gandhi. Both of them had that supreme spiritual quality which communicated itself to those near them. It was of course useless to argue with him about the rights of the Arabs and the wisdom of the Indian solution: but I did not hesitate to do so, because I felt that to talk to him was itself a privilege and any excuse which gave one that opportunity should not be missed. Moreover, in this case, the excuse was in itself something which tried to explore a path of peace.

One of the most moving scenes during that session of the General Assembly was when Dr. Weizmann personally appeared to testify before the political commission. The room was crowded to suffocation, for everyone in Lake Success felt that the occasion was historic. Slowly the imposing figure of the old Zionist leader, looking very much like an Old Testament prophet, appeared in the hall supported on both sides by younger men, for it was obvious that the strain was almost too great for him. It was only his iron will that enabled him to appear and plead the cause of his people before the assembled nations of the world. There was dead silence in the hall, and when the chairman called on him to speak, every ear was strained to hear what he had to say. It was difficult for him to read, as his sight was extremely bad; nor was his manner of speaking impressive, as he spoke English haltingly and with a strange accent. And yet everyone there felt the magnetism of his presence and realized that the old man who was addressing them stood for something which to him was more than all the riches of the world. From the personal point of view also the occasion had elements of high drama. The moment he had waited for, during the lifetime of incessant activity, had arrived. To few is it given to see the realization of their ideals in their own lifetime. To Chaim Weizmann it was a moment of triumph and yet he was in no mood of exaltation, but of humility. I called on him the next day at the Savoy Plaza to congratulate him personally, and I could see that he was deeply moved by the few words I addressed him.

There was one other matter of importance in which I was called on to play a minor part. While the Assembly was in session, the news had begun to appear in the American papers that a tribal invasion of Kashmir was in progress: that with the active assistance of Pakistan a large force of armed raiders had entered the territory of the State and that the Government of the Maharaja was about to collapse. The next day it became known that the raiders had entered the valley and were approaching Srinagar, the capital. The Indian delegation was gravely agitated by the news, but in the evening Mrs. Pandit received a personal telegram from the Prime Minister that, following the accession of the Maharaja to the Indian Union, supported by the largest political party in the State, troops had been flown to Srinagar and were in contact with the enemy.

The story of India's decision to intervene in Kashmir and to save the valley from the terrors of a tribal occupation is well known. But this unexpected move of the Indian Government came as a surprise to most Governments, who had, for some reason, assumed that Kashmir would go to Pakistan. There was suppressed excitement in United Nations circles as messages from New Delhi began to indicate that India was likely to charge Pakistan with aggression before the Security Council. Though the delegation had no information about this aspect of the question, Mrs. Pandit received a personal message from the Prime Minister asking her to get in touch with General Marshall, the American Secretary of State, and explain India's point of view to him. She was aware that I had been in Kashmir service at one time, and had since, in my work connected with the Chamber of Princes, kept myself fully informed with developments in that State. So she desired me not only to be present at the conversation, but to state the case for India.

George Marshall was on the point of departure for England for a conference, and he deputed Mr. Loy Henderson, later Ambassador to India, to visit Mrs. Pandit in New York and discuss the matter with her. I had in the meantime prepared a memorandum on the whole question. So when Mr. Henderson called on Mrs. Pandit at her hotel she asked me to explain the position of the Government of India, in relation not merely to the military action taken by us to meet the tribal attack, but the constitutional position arising from the accession of the Maharaja to the Indian Union. I also passed on to him the memorandum which I had prepared. This I believe was the first discussion between the representatives of U.S.A. and India on the Kashmir issue.

The developments in Kashmir, I felt satisfied, must have repercussions in other princely states, and the information reaching me about the situation in Bikaner where popular parties were pressing the Maharaja for the surrender of his autocratic powers made it necessary for me to return immediately to India. The work on the Third Committee had also finished and therefore with the permission of the Prime Minister I returned earlier than other delegates to India. I stopped a day in London and there I was able to pick up some very important information. At the Savoy Hotel where I was stopping, I met Colonel Waghre, who was in attendance on the Prince of Berar, and he told me of the heavy purchases of armament in which the Hyderabad Government was clandestinely engaged. He supplied me with the details of some of the transactions which could only have been meant for serious military action against India. It should be remembered that at this time the Indian Army was heavily engaged in Kashmir, and as a result of partition many of the units had not been fully reorganized. India was in a weak position militarily, a weakness which, as subsequent events were to show, the Nizam's advisers had exaggerated.

The first thing I did on reaching Delhi was to go to the Constituent Assembly, of which I was a member, and report to Vallabhai Patel, the Home Minister, the information I had gathered from Colonel Waghre. He took immediate action to stop the purchases in England and to prevent such purchases as had already been concluded from reaching Hyderabad. After a short stay in Bikaner I returned to Delhi to attend a meeting of the Foreign Affairs Committee of Parliament. After the meeting Nehru asked me very casually to go for a motor drive with him. I had no idea of what was coming. When we had driven on in silence for about ten minutes he asked rather abruptly: "Are you free to go abroad to take up an ambassador's post?" I replied that my work in Bikaner was coming to an end, and as soon as I could free myself from my commitments there I should be at his disposal for service anywhere. "When do you think you could get free?" he asked. "Say by the 1st of April," I replied. "Why not earlier, as the Maharaja is introducing popular government in the State?" I explained that, apart from having to tie up numerous loose ends in the State, I was anxious to continue my work on the committees of the Constituent Assembly to which I had been nominated. I calculated that these would have concluded their work by that time. I was a member of the committee on the Fundamental Principles of the Constitution, on Fundamental Rights, on the position of minorities and backward classes and many lesser bodies. Their reports had been completed, but had not been passed by the Constituent Assembly. When I expressed my desire to be associated with the last stages of our constitution making, the Prime Minister laughed. "It will take more time than you imagine. Since the committees have reported, the matter is now with the Constituent Assembly, and I do not think you need worry further about it. I should have liked you to be free earlier, but we can wait till April." There the conversation ended. It was characteristic of Nehru that he did not even say where I was to be posted. The next day Girja Shankar Bajpai, who was then Secretary-General of the Ministry of External Affairs, told me that the Prime Minister's intention was to post me to China.

Many people have claimed the credit for having suggested my name to the Prime Minister. Perhaps they did. I know that Nehru discussed the appointment with Mrs. Sarojini Naidu and Mrs. Pandit. I had worked with Nehru from 1924 to 1927 and he knew me fairly well at the time. We had again come together in connection with the work of securing the accession of the princely states to the constitution of India. Though I have never tried to find out, it is likely that the great affection in which I was held by Mrs. Sarojini Naidu, who always treated me as a member of her family, had also prejudiced him in my favour. In any case, as soon as the proposals were formalized, I felt it my duty to go to Lucknow where she was then residing as the Governor of the largest province in India and report the matter personally to her.

This was the last time I was to see this remarkable woman, one of the greatest that India has produced in her long history. A poet of high quality, an orator of unmatched eloquence, a national leader who had presided over the Indian National Congress in the days of its greatest power and influence, a woman of wit, charm and graciousness—above all a staunch friend and a very human and kind lady, Mrs. Naidu had dominated the life of intellectual India for a period of over forty years. She was the bridge between the old and the new. She had been the friend of Gokhale and was one of the earliest followers of Mahatma Gandhi. Her rooms, wherever she lived, were the meeting-place of vagabond poets, disreputable artists, society ladies, and national leaders. Everyone was welcome and to everyone she was Mother India. When she was in Delhi for the Constituent Assembly it had been my duty to escort her to Parliament House and back, and the day she left Delhi to take up her post as the Governor of the United Provinces the public demonstration at the Delhi railway station was one of the most enthusiastic.

In Lucknow, she kept court like a queen. The Muslim servants in the Government House, who had all been afraid of dismissal before she arrived to take charge, adored her. The great Muslim ladies of Lucknow—for centuries a centre of Muslim culture—found in her a protector and friend. Mrs. Naidu had one weakness: she dearly loved good food. Wherever her temporary abode was, her local admirers vied with each other in loading her table with rare, rich and unusual dishes. In Lucknow—renowned all over India for its delicious cooking—the Government House soon became the exhibition ground for the culinary triumphs of the great Nawabi families. During the three days that I stayed with her, there was not a meal when we were not served three or four dishes specially prepared and sent as tokens of affection by these noble ladies.

When I left Lucknow I knew in my heart of hearts that this was my last visit to the grand old lady. She had been ailing for over

B

eighteen months and yet had heroically carried on, her spirit refusing to yield to the increasing weakness of body. When I said goodbye to her, she gave me a message to Madame Sun Yat-sen and added: "I do not think I shall live to hear from you the stories of Cathay."

The Maharaja of Bikaner permitted me to retire from the Chief Ministership of the State on the 14th of March. I left the capital with many demonstrations of affection by the people of the State, some of whom accompanied me as far as Delhi and later on came to Calcutta to bid goodbye to me on my departure to China.

I was appointed as Ambassador attached to the External Affairs Ministry from the date of my resignation in Bikaner. A few days later the official agreement to my nomination was received from Nanking. I left Calcutta for China on the evening of the 13th of April, 1948, reaching Shanghai on the afternoon of the 14th. I had embarked on a career which was new and strange to me.

CHAPTER II

NANKING UNDER CHIANG KAI-SHEK

THE city of Shanghai, which was the first spot in China that I touched, was an unreal and fantastic creation. For nearly a hundred years it had been the metropolis of European business in the Far East, the symbol and pride of white superiority. To a large extent its glory had departed, for after the Japanese war, when the city was returned to the Chinese, all the paraphernalia of ex-territorial jurisdiction, consular courts, foreign policemen and the far-famed Municipal Council controlled by the Europeans, had vanished. Shanghai was no longer the sixth great power in the Far East, but merely the commercial capital of modern China. Bearded Sikhs no longer controlled the traffic on the *Bund*. The Mayor of the corporation and the Governor of the city was the celebrated K. C. Wu, a man of outstanding ability and recognized integrity. In spite of the brave front it maintained and the massive buildings on the *Bund*, the city had already begun to look a little dilapidated. An unending stream of refugees from North and Central China had flowed into Shanghai, and the first thing that struck me on arrival was the way that thousands of these poor people were allowed to wander about in the main streets.

I stayed in the city only for the day, for I was naturally anxious to reach the capital and take up my duties with as little delay as possible.

Nanking, to which Chiang Kai-shek had moved his capital for political and diplomatic reasons, is an old and attractive city. It is a strange combination of the old and the new, as most cities in China and India are. Some of the roads are wide and well laid out, while others are narrow, dirty and crowded beyond anything to be seen in India. Alongside the main streets one could see small patches of cultivation; and if in India cattle walk about, obstructing traffic, it was no unusual sight in Nanking to see hens and chickens crowding the streets. Nanking is a walled city and its walls are truly Cyclopean, a little less wide, I am told, than the more famous walls of Peking. Outside one of the gates lies the Lotus Lake, a place of enchanting beauty in summer with miles and miles of lotus flowers and islands with laid-out gardens, tea-houses, etc. The surroundings of Nanking are also very beautiful. A little outside lie the purple mountains with their Ming tombs, avenues of statuary and the curious old observatory. There also is situated the pretentious tomb which the Kuomintang erected in honour of its founder (Sun Yat-sen), a not unattractive building in the neo-classical style of China, which the party favoured at the time.

The embassy was situated in Peking Lu, and though the house was small and unsuitable for an embassy, it was in a good locality with a number of diplomatic residences near it. Opposite our house was the Egyptian Legation. The Portuguese Minister, Dr. Fonseca, resided nearby. But the more convenient houses were all occupied by American admirals and generals who were supposed to be advising the Kuomintang Government. Our house had some fine trees and a reasonable garden, and I had nothing much to complain of. The Burmese, Afghan, and Australian Embassies were at a convenient distance. So we were in a way well placed for work.

I was received with great kindness and courtesy both by the Chinese Government and by the diplomatic corps. The British Embassy and the other Commonwealth Missions were particularly anxious to show their friendliness as India was practically a newcomer in the diplomatic world. Sir Ralph Stevenson, H.B.M. Ambassador, made it clear to me from the beginning that I could look to him for friendly guidance in any difficulty. The Canadian Ambassador, T. C. Davies, was even more cordial. He was friendly and forthright and cared little for diplomatic conventions. His friendship which he frankly extended to me from the very first day was a source of great strength.

From the Chinese side, I was lucky that at the time of my arrival, Dr. Lo Chia-lun, whom I had known well in India, happened to be then in Nanking. In the Foreign Office I had a good friend in George Yeh, who was then Vice-Minister of Foreign Affairs. So my diplomatic barque was launched on smooth seas in fair weather with an immense amount of goodwill.

A few ambassadors and ministers had arrived just before me and were awaiting the presentation of credentials. Generalissimo Chiang Kai-shek therefore decided not to delay the ceremony any further and I was asked two days after my arrival by the Foreign Minister, Dr. Wang Shih-chieh, to send an advance copy of my speech. I was in a quandary as my letters of credence, which had to be signed by His Majesty in England, had not arrived. I mentioned this confidentially to George Yeh who made light of the matter and said that I could present a blank paper in an official-looking envelope and later deposit the credentials at the Foreign Office.

1 arrived in Nanking at a turning-point in the history of the Kuomintang. The capital was in the grip of unprecedented excitement following the meeting of the National Assembly. Under American pressure, General Chiang Kai-shek had reluctantly agreed to bring to a close the period of "military tutelage," which Sun Yat-sen, the founder of the Republic, had declared to be an essential period of preparation before the democratic constitution was introduced. So, after some prodding by General Marshall, Chiang Kai-shek had ordered nation-wide general elections. Though over large areas no elections took place and the pre-election agreements with the other parties were not honoured, a National Assembly had been constituted which claimed to represent the whole of China—including, it would seem, Tibet, whose representatives appeared in their national costume in the Assembly. The only function of the Assembly was to elect a President and a Vice-President. Law-making functions were with the Legislative Yuan, another body, while the right of general control and supervision was vested in the Control Yuan.

The question of the Presidency was agitating the public a great deal. There was a considerable body of opinion which felt that the time had come for General Chiang Kai-shek to retire and the general himself at one time seems to have thought that it was better for him to retire now, at the height of his glory, with all the prestige attaching to him as the victor in the war against Japan. He even went to the extent of announcing his intention of not putting himself forward as a candidate, and indeed suggested that Dr. Hu Shih would make an ideal President. But he seems to have been persuaded—perhaps not against his wishes—by Chen Li-fu, the head of the party organization and the evil genius of Chiang—to be "drafted" for the Presidency; and once he offered himself there was no question of anyone else being elected. The opposition therefore concentrated on the Vice-Presidency. The official candidate was Sun Fo, an unstable politician, who however enjoyed the prestige of being the son of the founder of the Republic, Sun Yat-sen. There were many other candidates for the post, but one on whom the hopes of the opposition rested was General Li Tsung-jen, the head of the Kwangsi faction who had been a life-long opponent of Chiang. General Li, with the support of his friend and associate, the Muslim war lord, Pai Chung-hsi, had defied Chiang for many years before the Japanese war and had established an independent government in Kwangsi. At the time of national unity against the Japanese he had returned to his allegiance; but his own great abilities as a general, friendship with Pai Chung-hsi, the most brilliant of the Kuomintang commanders, and their joint hold on a vital province in the south had made him a rival rather than a subordinate of Chiang. General Li was credited with liberal opinions: at least the American Embassy thought so. He was personally considered an honest man—an exceptional thing among the military leaders of the Kuomintang. Much pressure was put on him by Chiang to retire from the contest, but with the encouragement of the Americans who distrusted Sun Fo he held on and was elected with a great majority. This was the first political defeat of General Chiang Kai-shek and it had tremendous effect on the events of the next twelve months.

Sun Fo had to be content with the Presidentship of the Legislative Yuan, an ineffective Parliament which was entrusted with the duty of legislation. The Control Yuan, the successor of the Imperial Board of Censors, elected Yu Yu-jen, a pre-Kuomintang revolutionary and one of the leaders of the 1912 movement as President. Tai Chi-tao, a staunch Buddhist, one of the founding members of the communist party, who later recanted, and one-time leader of the anti-Christian federation, presided over the Examination Yuan. On the whole it may be said that this experiment in pseudo-parliamentary institutions did not work out as Chiang Kai-shek had expected, or as the party bosses, the Chen brothers, had assured him that it would. The elections were almost universally interpreted as an expression of no confidence in the "C. C. Clique" of which Chen Li-fu was the head. Chiang, recognizing the writing on the wall, gave Chen Li-fu permission to leave for a tour of instruction in America and Europe, a courteous method of dismissal. Chen Li-fu appeared in America a few months later as the leader of the Chinese delegation to Dr. Buchman's moral rearmament conference.

The installation of Chiang Kai-shek was the first public ceremony that I had to attend in China. It was done with imposing pageantry, and the Generalissimo, after being invested with the office of the President of the Chinese Republic, delivered a speech in which he promised in all solemnity to exterminate the communist forces within a period of three months! Everyone felt happy, and the Americans, and to a lesser extent the British, felt that China was now well set on a road to democratic evolution. There was a great deal of mutual congratulation and no one seemed in the least worried about the People's Liberation Army or the regime that Mao Tse-tung had established in inaccessible regions.

The first indication that all was not well with the new regime was the sulky way in which the new Vice-President behaved. He ostentatiously washed his hands of the regime and after a few weeks of stay in the capital quietly slipped out and took up his residence in Peking under the protection of his friend, General Fu Tso-yi, who was the representative of the Central Government at Peking and was responsible for the defence of North China.

However, these facts did not worry me greatly at the time. What did cause me grave concern was the state of exchange and consequently of my own finances. The Fa Pi or the National Chinese dollar was falling so rapidly that money was fast losing value. The official rate of exchange bore no relation to the actual rates and a suitcase full of notes was required for an ordinary shopping. Most of the embassies were not troubled about this, as they were well supplied with American dollars, which had become the unofficial currency of the country. But the Government of India was adamant on this matter and refused, in view of its own dollar shortage, to supply us with any currency other than the rupee which had to be changed at a loss of over sixty per cent at official rates. The effects of inflation were indeed fantastic. China was then the one place in the world where there were no controls of any kind. Everything was available and could be purchased at very reasonable prices if payment was made in American dollars. In Chinese currency or at official rates the prices were fantastically high. In all public places American currency could be openly bought and sold, and even some of the highest officials of the Chinese Government were known to have indulged in this practice. In fact one very distinguished officer who had let his house to my military attaché insisted on the rent being paid every month in American dollars, and on our pointing out that we had no dollars agreed finally as a compromise to be paid in rupees.

The misery of the people was unbelievable, for currency rates changed from hour to hour. The servants were paid according to a complicated system based on the cost of living index calculated every fortnight (by the British Embassy). As soon as they received their wages, they used to rush out and buy their rice and other requirements for the fortnight.

Apart from the inconveniences arising out of this inflation, life in Nanking was extremely pleasant. During the first two months of my stay there, the leading personalities of the country were in Nanking for the National Assembly. I had therefore an opportunity of meeting some of them and discussing matters generally. I came to know well Dr. Hu Shih, the celebrated scholar who was at the time the President of the Peking National University, Dr. S. R. Chow, well known as an expert in international law, and others whom I had previously met in New York or London. There were many high officials who were men of outstanding ability and culture; men like Wang Shih-chieh, the Foreign Minister, Yu Ta-wei, a remarkable personality, a scholar and a scientist, who was then the Minister of Transport. George Yeh, the Vice Foreign Minister, and Dr. Wu, who was the principal of the famous Ginling College for women, where my daughter had been admitted as a boarder.

I also had opportunities of meeting General Chiang Kai-shek and his wife Madame Chiang (Soong Mei-ling). They were particularly kind to us and more than once invited us to dine with them *en famille*. General Chiang struck me as a very masterful personality, a patriot and leader who thought always in terms of the greatness of China, which he no doubt honestly equated with his own leadership. He was simple in his habits and almost austere in his life. No one has ever accused him of personal corruption. Public criticism was mainly directed against those who surrounded him, including some members of his immediate family.

Chiang Kai-shek was a great man who was born a century too late. He had all the qualities which in earlier periods would have inevitably led him to establish a new dynasty and give a new lease of life to the old traditions of China. Chiang was not a mandarin and had indeed no pretensions to scholarship. He was and remained a peasant and to some extent that was his strength. He was nominally a Christian (Methodist) and I am told used to preach every Sunday to a select group who gathered in his private chapel. But the Methodist preacher had also become the champion of a new Confucianism, with an ardent faith in the traditions of China. In fact he was a mass of contradictions—a Christian who believed in Confucianism, a democratic president who believed in military dictatorship, a scrupulously honest man who tolerated large-scale corruption among the people who surrounded him.

Madame Chiang was a personage of a totally different character. Beautiful and elegant, well educated and with wide knowledge of affairs, she gave one the impression of immense vitality and great determination. She was endowed by nature with the manners of a person conscious of her own superiority: and no doubt as a result of being for many years the first lady of the land, she had also developed the deportment of a queen! But the General and Madame had been strong supporters of the national movement in India and were genuinely pleased when India became independent. So in her treatment of us she showed a natural cordiality, but so far as the diplomatic corps was generally concerned she was distant and aloof, an Olympian moving in rarefied heights. The first time she received my wife and myself was at an informal party at the Presidency to which the Burmese Ambassador and his wife, the Greek Ambassador and the Philippine Minister and his wife were also invited. The Greek Ambassador, who claimed to be an expert on Chinese ceramics and bronzes, entered into a long conversation with the Generalissimo on art in the Far East—a subject in which the General was not at all interested—and gave him a description of the great Chinese collection that he had left behind in Athens. The only reaction of the General was an occasional "Ocho!" which I understood meant "good" in the Chekiang dialect which the Generalissimo spoke. The Philippine Minister, his wife and two daughters explained the intricacies of what they called the Philippine national dress to Madame Chiang and generously promised to present her with one. To me it appeared that the so-called "national" dress of the Philippines was nothing more than a colonial and tropical variation of nineteenth-century Spanish dress and Madame Chiang herself seemed greatly amused at this emphasis on its national character. She remarked smilingly that the dress of each country suited the people and climate of the country and turned to my wife and said that during her visit to India she had been presented with a number of saris by Mrs. Pandit and others, but that she had never a chance of wearing them. Conversation with the General was more difficult, as he had very little to say on any subject. He, however, asked me a few questions about Pandit Nehru and how things were going on in Kashmir, etc.—just enough to indicate to me his deep interest in India.

It did not take me long to discover that the Kuomintang attitude towards India, while genuinely friendly, was inclined to be a little patronizing. It was the attitude of an elder brother who was considerably older and well established in the world, prepared to give his advice to a younger brother struggling to make his way. Independence of India was welcome, but of course it was under-stood that China as the recognized Great Power in the East after the war expected India to know her place. The Foreign Office or the Wai Chiaopu was the best organized department of the Government and it was here that this doctrine was most firmly held. It seemed strange to me that Kuomintang China, dependent as she was for almost everything—even her Great Power status— on America, should take up this attitude. But soon I realized that even in regard to America the attitude of China was one of patronizing condescension. China accepted financial and other help as her due, with the attitude of a great nobleman permitting himself to be assisted in a crisis by a newly-rich neighbour. To the Kuomintang, which had inherited the mantle of the Son of Heaven, America was no more than the great barbarian for whose dollars and equipment she had immediate need, but for whose culture she had no great admiration. Chiang himself was in no sense a pro-American, while those around him like Chen Pu-li and Chen Li-fu were aggressive Confucians who believed in the racial and moral superiority of the Chinese. Madame Chiang, brought up in an American college and with a Christian family background, lived in a half world. She was for all outward appearance and behaviour completely Europeanized, but I suspect that in her also there was a strain of racial pride which made her resent the American attitude.

The behaviour of the American colony in Nanking was generally speaking not such as to evoke feelings of friendliness on the part of the Chinese. By a process known as Lend-Lease in reverse the best sites in Nanking were taken over by the Americans. The residence of the pro-Japanese President Wang Ching-wei with its extensive gardens was converted into the American club. The best houses had been requisitioned for the American generals and other experts. Refrigerators, radio sets and other useful things imported into China without payment of customs duty began to reappear in the market on a fairly large scale and rumours were afloat of scandalous behaviour towards women. One such incident in which a woman student in the Peking University was said to have been assaulted by a GI created almost a national crisis. On top of it, suspicion began to grow in official circles and in non-official political groups that under MacArthur's leadership America was building up Japan again. On the whole, relations between the Kuomintang and the Americans were not as friendly as people imagined: but the Chinese realized that they could not get on without the Americans and the Americans on their part realized that the success of their Asian policy depended on a firm alliance with China. It was, however, not a happy union.

After spending some time in Nanking, I went on an official visit to Shanghai. Shanghai was still the financial and commercial metropolis of China, where India had opened a Consulate-General. Also, we had at that time a considerable Indian population, consisting mostly of Sikhs, who had in the days of British authority been employed as policemen under the Municipality, but who had settled down as watchmen in business firms. There was also a sprinkling of businessmen, old-established firms of Parsis, new Gujerati merchants, and others. Apart from visiting the Indian community and establishing contacts with the officials, I was also desirous of meeting Madame Sun Yat-sen, to whom Pandit Nehru had given me a letter. Madame Sun was not in favour with Chiang's Government. In fact she was living under close surveillance in Shanghai and it was generally believed that she was not allowed to move out of that city. But in Shanghai itself she held court like a queen, visited often by leading foreign personalities in the city and managing numerous public charities. It was widely suspected even at that time that she was in secret communication with Mao Tse-tung and that her sympathies were with the communists. In any case she made no secret of the fact that her sympathies were not with the Kuomintang.

She received me and my family with the greatest cordiality and talked to us a great deal about Indian personalities she had met at different times. She also spoke to me about her work among the refugees and about the schools and institutions which she was running for the children in the refugee camps. One of her assistants in this work was Dr. Anna Wang, a German lady who was married to Wang Ping-nan of the communist armies. In her company we visited the schools, clinical centres, children's theatres and other cultural activities which were directed by

Madame Sun. It was clear to me that this was only an interim activity for her, that she was patiently waiting for the day when things would be different and she would have again a great part to play in national affairs.

Soong Chin-ling (Madame Sun) was altogether different from her sister, Soong Mei-ling (Madame Chiang). Madame Sun had a graciousness, poise, and dignity which her more vital sister lacked. She was a grand lady, not by her manner or by her airs, but by nature. She spoke quietly and in soft tones and there was around her a general atmosphere of serenity. She was in fact serene. She had none of the vivaciousness of Sarojini Naidu, none of her brilliance. Nor did she convey the sense of homely intimacy which even a first visit to Mrs. Naidu gave to her visitors. Also, she did not give the impression of extraordinary energy and vitality which are natural to Madame Chiang. But no one who has been in the presence of Madame Sun would deny her natural graciousness, her serenity, and her charm, which, combined with a remarkable earnestness of spirit and an unswerving loyalty to political principles, made her one of the greatest women of our time.

Shanghai was then enjoying its sunset glow. No longer was it the proud Queen of the Pacific, dictating the policy of nations with interests in China. Its great municipality, elected by foreign ratepayers, who had, under the protection of extra-territoriality and the immense profits of the China trade, built up this megalopolis, had given place after the war to Chinese administration. The suave K. C. Wu, ably assisted by his secretary (Pearl Chen), was now the Mayor of Shanghai. And yet some of the outward symbols of foreign domination had continued. In the centre of the city was situated a great racecourse, without which it is difficult for Englishmen to live in foreign countries. On the *Bund* itself was situated the Shanghai Club, which was reputed to have the longest bar in the world where at lunch-time streamed in the great ones of British business. The country clubs, English, French and Italian, with extensive grounds and luxurious apartments in the commercial heart of China, proclaimed the importance of the different European communities. In fact, Shanghai at that time still had over 60,000 European inhabitants and was undoubtedly the largest European city outside Europe. This was for them a period of unexampled prosperity.

But their authority over the city had gone and no one knew where exactly the authority was vested. There was of course the Mayoral Government of K. C. Wu, but it was known that behind and above him loomed the sinister Tu Yen-shen, a notorious gangster and dope king, who had by a process known to few emerged after the war as a philanthropist and a highly respected dignitary of Shanghai. Tu's career is one of the romances of Shanghai, indeed of modern China. Born in the slums of the French concession, Tu worked at different trades, orange seller, dope trafficker and general tough man, gradually assuming a more and more important role in the underworld of Shanghai. Sometime in his career he joined the powerful secret society of Green Shirts, which exercised such immense power in China. He became one of the Elders of this society and there came into contact with a junior initiate, Chiang Kai-shek, who in the period between 1915 and 1923 was at a loose end and was earning a living, it is said, as a bartender. Whatever be the truth in regard to this, there is no doubt of the immense hold that Tu Yen-shen came to have on Chiang all the time the former was alive.

When Chiang's armies reached the outskirts of Shanghai and there was every possibility of a rising in the city, it was to Tu that the French turned. Through his efforts the French concession was calm and peaceful. But in the international concession a great revolt, organized by the communists, with Chou En-lai as deputy commander, had broken out. This was against the policy of Chiang who had made up his mind to break with his communist allies. It was to his Elder Brother in the Secret Society, Tu, that Chiang turned at the crisis, and it was through the influence of Tu, who threw the organized power of the Secret Societies and Guilds into the scale against the communists, that the revolution was suppressed.

After the establishment of the Kuomintang Government in Nanking, Tu's power and influence in Shanghai was more or less openly exercised. But he had the wisdom not to leave his French protectors, who even honoured him with a decoration for his services during the crisis. From 1926 to 1936 Tu Yen-shen was the most powerful Chinese in the city. He was, however, an unseen force, a kind of Fu Manchu who operated from behind the scenes, with a share in all the underworld activities for which Shanghai became notorious during this period. When the Japanese occupied Shanghai, Tu continued to stay in the French concession and was of great assistance to the nationalists in keeping their communications open with the population in the city. George Yeh himself told me that when he was once caught in the Japanese-occupied area, it was Tu who arranged for his escape.

After the war, when Shanghai was retroceded to China, Tu Yen-shen came to be accepted even in high society as one of the great figures of the city. He was generally described in the newspapers as the great philanthropist. In appearance he looked a distinguished old-style mandarin, a grave, benevolent personality, courteous and dignified, one who looked on the affairs of the world with a friendly detachment.

While the business in the city seemed flourishing, and an unending line of rickshaws and pedicabs streamed through the city streets during day time, and neon lights blazed at night, and taxi dancers and dope pedlars found their paradise in innumerable dens and night clubs, even a casual observer could have seen that death had begun to cast its shadow on the place. The streets were crowded with beggars. Refugees were dying like rats and no one seemed to care about their fate. Black market flourished openly and all civic sense had departed. The mayor, K. C. Wu, fought valiantly to maintain some kind of order, but confessed himself to be helpless. It was a dreadful situation and I returned to the less exciting life in Nanking with a sense of intense relief.

CHAPTER III

THE COLLAPSE OF THE NANKING REGIME

IN July the Government decided at last on a plan of currency reform. A new currency called the Gold Yuan was introduced and the old Fa Pi was withdrawn from circulation. It was announced that the new currency was fully backed by gold and that every known precaution would be taken to see that it did not depreciate. As an earnest of their intention to give effect to this programme, the Government appointed Chiang Ching-kuo, the son of General Chiang Kai-shek who was well known for his integrity and fearlessness, as enforcing officer in Shanghai. Young Chiang was given unlimited powers to deal summarily with everyone, regardless of rank and position, and to put right the economic life of the city. Chiang Ching-kuo went about it with a soldierly forthrightness which struck terror into the hearts of black-marketeers, currency speculators and all others who were interested in illegal transactions. For over four weeks Shanghai was practically terror-stricken into good behaviour, but Tiger Chiang soon came up against the unseen might of Tu's underground empire. One of the people arrested by Chiang Ching-kuo and hauled up before the special tribunal was a recognized agent of Tu, and Tiger Chiang in arresting him was deliberately challenging Tu's power. Everyone in China knew that the battle had been joined and that the future of the currency depended upon the outcome. The situation was really tense. Tu waited patiently for a short time hoping that young Chiang would come to his senses, but when the Tiger showed no signs of relenting, quietly travelled up to Nanking. The mighty Generalissimo compromised and Tu's agent was let off with a nominal punishment.

Almost at the same time Tiger Chiang had come up against an

equally powerful enemy. His agents had unearthed an enormous store of prohibited goods in the godowns of the Yangtse Development Corporation which was controlled by no less a person than H. H. Kung, whose wife was the elder sister of Madame Chiang Kai-shek. David Kung, H. H. Kung's son and Madame Chiang's nephew, was in charge of the business and the Tiger not only raided the premises and took possession of the store, but threatened to arrest David Kung himself. The young man telephoned his aunt. My wife and myself happened to be dining with the Generalissimo when the call came through and madame left the table to receive the message. When she came back she was looking thunder and lightning. She brusquely stated that she was leaving for Shanghai early in the morning. I did not then know what the matter was, but on returning home, I sent a message to my Consul-General in Shanghai to try and discover the object of madame's sudden visit to the city. I need not have troubled at all, for the whole of China knew by next evening that Madame Chiang had decisively intervened against her stepson and told him that he was overstepping the bounds of his authority in attacking the Kung interests. A few days later David Kung left for America in circumstances which created a great scandal in the country.

Thus ended the fight for currency stability. Chiang Ching-kuo gave up his post in disgust and it then became clear that the Gold Yuan would go the way of the Fa Pi, which it had displaced. The crash came a few days later when I happened to be in Peking.

During the course of the dinner with the Generalissimo alluded to above, he asked me whether I had so far visited Peking. I replied that I was hoping to go within a few days. He was good enough then to offer me the use of a private plane which I gratefully accepted. Two weeks later I flew to the northern capital, as it then was. I had then no idea that the crisis in the civil war which in the course of six months was to sweep Chiang away from his capital was so near. Everything seemed normal when we left Nanking in the morning. In the afternoon when we arrived in Peking the atmosphere was tense. News had just reached Peking that Tsinan, one of the great provincial capitals, had fallen to the communists—the first city to be taken by them. The effect of this item of news

c

was paralysing. Everyone in the Wagons-lit Hotel, where we were staying, discussed only one topic: whether the communists would now attack Peking. The city had lived in a state of terror, as the communists were present in force less than fifty miles away: but it had been the general idea that they did not have the strength to capture and hold big cities. Indeed they had shown no inclination to do so and therefore the occupation of Tsinan came as a great shock.

Peking is a city of great beauty. It has the atmosphere of a great imperial capital. The "forbidden city" with its yellow tiled roofs shining like gold, covering an immense area and dominating the capital, the great lakes with pleasure gardens and artificial hills, the low-roofed houses, with endless courtyards, pools and rock gardens, the Cyclopean walls with their imposing gates and drum towers—all these cannot fail to impress even a visitor familiar with sights of London, Paris, and New York. But its condition was pitiable when we saw it for the first time. Peking had been deliberately neglected for a period of over two decades. I was told that the grant for the upkeep of the Forbidden City was not sufficient to pay the sweepers. The beautiful lakes were full of weeds, dirty and uncared for. Refugees from communist-occupied areas had forcibly taken possession of the world-famous monuments of the city and were living there huddled up, without sanitary arrangements, or even elementary precautions of cleanliness. In the Temple of Heaven, universally recognized to be one of the most beautiful buildings in the world, more than a thousand students were living just as they liked, more than fifty of them sleeping in the robing room of the Son of Heaven. The filth which covered the sacred grounds was indescribable. Nor was the Temple of Confucius or the Hall of Classics spared by them. It was altogether a painful sight. I mentioned this to the municipal authorities when I called on the mayor and his reply was: "These young men who ought to be at the front consider themselves our masters. My authority does not extend to them. There is nothing to stop them from taking over any other building if they choose." While this no doubt was the position in regard to the civil authorities, the military rulers of Peking were not so easy to handle. The supreme command in this area was vested in the famous General Fu Tso-yi, then considered by the Americans as the sole hope of the Kuomintang forces in the north. The Americans had been for some time pressing the Generalissimo to permit them to supply Fu Tso-yi direct, as the latter had been complaining that Chiang was keeping him in short supply. Chiang of course knew his man better, as later events proved. When the American supplies were directly delivered to him, Fu Tso-yi's stock stood high. He was undoubtedly a very efficient soldier. I did not have the opportunity of meeting him, as he was at the front when I was there, but his deputy entertained me to a formal dinner at the former Japanese Embassy. We were received in the historic room, where the notorious twenty-one demands were forced on the Chinese, and the dinner served to us was of a most sumptuous kind. There we heard all about the plans to destroy in one sweep the communist swarms which surrounded Peking. The very next day, however, I had some information which gave me an inkling of how things were shaping. A colleague of mine—an important representative of one of the Western powers—told me in conversation that he had put through a deal with the communists in Peking itself and that a "group" in his country was supplying arms worth millions of pounds to the communists. I was taken aback and asked him how he was able to do it under the very nose of Fu Tso-yi. He only winked and said everything could be arranged! As in another three months Fu Tso-yi went over to Mao Tse-tung, it was clear that things had been arranged.

The famous Peita University had invited me to deliver a course of lectures, and the other academic institutions in Peking had also been generous with their hospitality. This brought me into contact with the intellectuals in the city, and as Dr. Hu Shih, though he was away lecturing in another university, had written to his friends, I was received by them with great cordiality and kindness. The conditions under which the professors lived were appalling. They got no more than a pittance, which was supplemented with a grant of rice! Literally, most of them did not get sufficient to eat or to clothe themselves decently; and yet they struggled on heroically to keep up the academic traditions of China. No wonder that most of them were discontented, and I suspected that in the case of a good few their sympathies were with Mao Tse-tung. Many of the younger leaders in the communist camp, e.g. Po Yi-po, were students who had crossed over at one time or another to the communist camp, and I was told by teachers in the university that there was a regular exodus of senior students in batches to the communist areas a few miles outside the city. Another strange fact was that the sympathy of the foreign professors seemed to lie mainly with the communists.

I stayed in Peking for twelve days. The last two days of my stay witnessed a remarkable development. It was known locally as the "buying spree." It was a kind of moral epidemic under the influence of which almost everyone in the city with any cash rushed to the shops to buy anything that was available. A Chinese acquaintance of mine went from shop to shop buying watches: another concentrated on fountain-pens. In fact all that people seemed anxious to do was to get rid of the paper money they had and lay their hands on something which was substantial. It was clear that the Gold Yuan on which such hopes had been built up was going the way of its predecessor. The reason for this sudden collapse was not obvious, unless it be that the public had somehow come to guess what the censorship had been effectively concealing so far, that is, the disastrous development in Manchuria.

While we were in Peking Chiang Kai-shek himself had arrived there and after a hurried consultation flown to Mukden. There he called together commanders of the area and decided on a plan of action which was to eliminate the powerful communist forces under General Lin Piao, which had taken over the countryside. Before actual fighting started in Manchuria, we returned to Nanking in order to be present in the capital for the "double tenth"—the 10th of October—which the Kuomintang celebrated as the national day. This year, however, there were no celebrations. The news had begun to trickle down that the Manchurian armies, the best that Chiang had from the point of leadership, training and equipment, had been surrounded by Lin Piao and were surrendering in large numbers. The Manchurian campaign was fast ending in total disaster and it was clear that North China also would not be able to hold out much longer. The "double tenth" was therefore celebrated in an atmosphere of gloom.

The pressure on Chiang Kai-shek to relax his control on the administration began to increase. This came from many different quarters—the army, the politicians, liberal thinkers, and even high officials. One strange and unexpected development was the position that the Legislative Yuan, or Parliament, began to assume. Under the Kuomintang-sponsored constitution, Government was not responsible to the Legislative Yuan, but this body began effectively to voice popular discontent and make Chiang's administration difficult. It adopted a policy of criticizing everything and everybody and indirectly challenging the Generalissimo's prerogative of appointing the Cabinet. The Prime Minister, Wong Wen-hao, had resigned, but the Legislative Yuan kept on obstructing the appointment of anyone suggested by Chiang. They were vociferous in their demand for peace, for ending the civil war. The Control Yuan, which was vested with the authority for seeing that the constitution was adhered to and had also the right of direct enquiry into administrative scandals, began directly to take up matters discrediting Chiang or those near him. Months after David Kung had departed for America following Chiang Ching-kuo's action against the Yangtse Development Corporation, the Control Yuan insisted on an enquiry, the object of which was to attack and discredit Madame Chiang Kai-shek. It became obvious during the weeks following the double tenth (October 1948) that there was mounting opposition to the Generalissimo and his regime and that a widespread popular movement for peace was developing in the country.

Chiang's reaction to this growing opposition was characteristic. He made another speech promising to annihilate the communists finally in another three months. When in May he had made a similar announcement it did not sound improbable, nor was it taken as a wild claim by the general public. In May the communist areas were undefined and though everyone knew that Mao Tse-tung controlled a powerful army, it had not so far fought a decisive action. The communists could not then claim undivided authority even over a single province. They roamed over large

areas, but every town of importance and most provinces were
under the control of the Central Government, which then disposed
of a well-equipped army of over four million people, some
units of which had been trained by the Americans and had had a
great deal of battle experience in Burma. But in November it
looked a vain boast, for not only had Chiang's Manchurian armies,
numbering near a million, been lost to him, together with the
north-eastern provinces, but Peking and Tientsin had come under
attack with but little chance of effective defence. More, the
redoubtable generals, Liu Po-cheng, known as the one-eyed
dragon, and the hard-hitting Chen Yi, had appeared before
Hsuchow, which everyone recognized to be the gateway to
Nanking. A great battle had been joined at Hsuchow, which, if
lost by Chiang's forces, would seal the fate of Nanking and
indeed of the Kuomintang Government. Chiang threw all his
available forces into this battle and is said to have himself taken
long-distance control of the operations. A great battle of encircle-
ment and annihilation went on for over a month, the only serious
battle in the civil war. The result was decisive; Chiang's forces
were beaten and the victory lay with the communists.

Internally also the situation was cracking up. Before Chiang
entered upon the Hsuchow campaign he had embarked on a policy
of repression. In the universities, hotbeds of anti-Chiang agitation,
the Kuomintang Youth Corps, a fascist gang masquerading as
students, had orders to beat up all malcontents. Security measures
had been tightened and talk of peace was declared unpatriotic and
treasonable. But these measures had but little effect. The Legislative Yuan had become the mouthpiece of the opposition and the
Americans were banking on these beginnings of democracy.
Chiang found his hands tied in dealing with this body. In fact the
American Embassy itself had slowly veered round to a cautious
support of Li Tsung-jen, the Vice-President, and was informally
putting it out that the only way of safety lay in Chiang's withdrawal.

A violent anti-American agitation had also broken out at the
same time. The remarkable recovery of Japanese economy and
MacArthur's open plea that Japan should be strengthened as a

counterweight to the growing communist power on the mainland had given the public sufficient ground for working up a great agitation. It is clear now that it must have been communist inspired, but wherever the inspiration came from, it was taken up by practically all sections of the public. The Government itself had to issue statements. The attitude of the American Consul-General in Shanghai who declared this agitation to be an act of ingratitude, and leading articles in the American-owned Shanghai *Evening News*, generally voicing contempt for the Chinese, did not help matters. The American Embassy, caught between the fires of anti-Americanism and of the suspicion of being staunch champions of Chiang, began to waver and to give cautious support to the liberals.

With the fall of Hsuchow and Pengpu, Chiang's position became untenable. The only undefeated army of any strength was under the command of Pai Chung-hsi, the Muslim General, who was the close friend and associate of the Vice-President. Pai, whose headquarters were at Hankow, had refused to allow his troops to be thrown into the battle of Hsuchow. When, after the disastrous outcome of that battle, Chiang called a conference of his military commanders and provincial governors to meet him in Nanking, very few took the trouble to come. This "epidemic of polite disobedience," as it was described in the Chinese papers, convinced Chiang, more than anything else, that it was time for him to retire, at least temporarily.

It was when the situation was developing this way that my wife one evening received from Madame Chiang Kai-shek a present of a bunch of the most beautiful chrysanthemums. We considered this strange and rang up Madame Meyrier at the French Embassy to find out whether she had also received a present of a similar nature. As it happened a similar gift had been sent to her and, I heard, also to the wife of another ambassador. It was only the next morning when the newspapers announced the fact that Madame Chiang had left for America that we recognized the significance of this gracious act.

The clamour for peace kept mounting. General Chang Chih-chun, who had been one of the most trusted officers of the Generalissimo and represented him in the strategic north-west provinces, including Sinkiang, suddenly arrived in Nanking as the champion of the peace party. He came to call on me and when I asked him how long he intended to stay on in Nanking, his reply was "till everything is settled." Chang Chih-chun, I guessed, was already in contact with the communist authorities, many of whom he knew intimately. In fact he had been one of the representatives of Chiang Kai-shek in the negotiations with the communists during General Marshall's mediation. Unlike other advocates of peace he made no speeches, but it was clear that he intended to force the issue with the Generalissimo.

Finally the Generalissimo gave in. One reason for his abrupt decision, I was told, was the failure of his wife's mission to America. The State Department had frankly cold-shouldered her and no promises of immediate help were held out. Betrayed at home by his own generals, and abroad by those whom he considered his friends, Chiang agreed reluctantly to step down and hand over power to Li Tsung-jen as Acting President. He then left for his home province of Chekiang on a Confucian pilgrimage to his mother's tomb.

Looking back on the events briefly described above I have not the least doubt that the Generalissimo's surrender of leadership at this time was one of the major factors that brought about the sudden collapse of the Kuomintang. Chiang was the only man around whom the defence of the Kuomintang cause could have been organized. He alone enjoyed sufficient authority and prestige in the army and among the people in the nationalist areas. Also he alone had the determination, the unbending resolve not to yield. But the fact was that a mood of defeatism had swept over the middle classes and the intellectuals who felt convinced that the civil war—the fight between brother and brother—could be brought to an honourable end through negotiations. A powerful group in Parliament saw in Chiang the major obstacle to the negotiations and concentrated their fire on him. Also the communist radio kept on emphasizing that but for foreign influences—American—unity and peace would have reigned in China long ago. So from about the middle of November Chiang had foreseen the possibility that he might have to retire. He began building up in Formosa the funds, equipment and other requirements for continued resistance. MacArthur, then playing the Mikado in Japan, was determined to keep Formosa out of communist control. So, one day quietly and without fuss the Generalissimo withdrew after issuing a proclamation which made it clear that he reserved for himself the right to resume the Presidency whenever he thought it proper. It was not a resignation, but a temporary withdrawal.

Li Tsung-jen who thus became the Acting President was an amiable gentleman with an ambitious wife who was intensely jealous of Madame Chiang Kai-shek. Li inaugurated his regime with a number of liberal decrees—one abolished the dreaded secret police; another freed political opponents who had been rotting in jail for years. A third suppressed the Kuomintang youth organizations which had terrorized the universities. But all these well-meaning measures remained ineffective. The secret police was responsible only to Chiang and worked under his orders. "The young Marshal," Chang Hsueh-liang, the son of the Manchurian war lord Chang Tso-lin, who had been confined in some unknown place for his part in the Sian incident, continued to remain in jail in spite of the clear orders of the Acting President. The army commanders took no notice of General Li and looked to Chiang's agents for their orders. In fact there was utter confusion in Nanking.

In this difficulty Li had to depend more and more on Parliament, where the peace group had gained greatly in strength as a result of Chiang's withdrawal. The pressure for direct negotiations became greater every day, while the will to resist declined proportionately. Finally when the communist armies had reached Pukow on the Yangtse, opposite Nanking itself, Li Tsung-jen addressed a telegram to Mao Tse-tung offering to negotiate a settlement. The communist leaders, who were fully informed of the rapid political disintegration in Nanking, welcomed the move and put forward an eight-point basis for negotiations.

The situation in Nanking was bordering on anarchy. One morning the American Military Advisory group and high military and naval officials attached to the Nanking administration went away without much warning. This was of course interpreted by the people as a sure indication that the war had been lost! I was suddenly faced with a rather difficult problem. The Americans had recruited and employed over 150 Indians as Military Police. They were a trained and disciplined body of men. Suddenly, with the departure of their American employers, these people were not only left without employment but with no prospects of return to India. As the Americans had recruited them in China, no arrangements had been made for their repatriation. Naturally they turned to me in this difficulty. As the general situation was deteriorating rapidly I did not know what to do with this 150 ex-soldiers, who, as it appeared, were also supplied with American arms. Then an idea struck me. The embassies in Nanking had generally taken alarm at the growing inadequacy of police arrangements in the city. Many instances of well-planned burglaries in embassies had also been reported. The British Embassy officials, with their accustomed foresight, were also considering measures in case the city came under siege. An elaborate scheme for evacuating the Commonwealth diplomats and personnel had been worked out. Arrangements had also been made to put in ample stock of foodstuffs. The central point of the scheme was that a British man-of-war would be anchored at Nanking, in which all of us would go down the Yangtse under the protection of the guns of the Royal Navy. Every week a new destroyer sailed up the river, and the rival Chinese forces on both banks of the Yangtse could see that the Commonwealth nationals in any case had at least the symbolic protection of the Navy. Everyone was satisfied that the communists would not dare to alienate the British by firing on the destroyer, especially when the Pacific fleet was at hand and, it was thought, could sail up easily and patrol the Yangtse as before. How mistaken these calculations were, events were soon to prove. But in February we all had a comfortable feeling of security, with the clock-like arrival of British and Australian destroyers, whose officers and men we felt happy to fête and entertain.

There was, however, one weakness in this scheme. There was no arrangement for protection inside the city in case law and order completely broke down and the more dangerous elements among the underworld took over. Previous experience of massacres of foreigners, the destruction of their property and the desecration of their churches, rankled in most European minds and there was a genuine fear that if there was a siege of Nanking foreign lives might not be safe. When this matter came up for discussion, it struck me that the disbanded American Military Police could be organized as a private force and entrusted with the responsibility of guarding the Commonwealth embassies. I undertook to do so, if the other Commonwealth Missions agreed to contribute proportionately to the expenditure. This they were only too happy to do and within two days I was able to inspect a private army of my own, which took over the guard duties of the embassies and of the residences of senior diplomatic personnel. Till the communists actually crossed over on the 23rd of April these guards functioned publicly, and their bearing, behaviour and discipline elicited universal admiration. Even after the communists took over, they were not disbanded immediately. They were, however, asked to remain within the embassy compounds and generally to keep themselves in the background. But they were there, and in a small way they gave to the Commonwealth community a sense of personal security which all of them appreciated.

General Li, after some prevarication, mainly due to the fact that he was being subjected to contradictory advice, finally decided to send a delegation to Peking to discuss the terms of peace on the basis of the eight points which Mao Tse-tung had put forward. An unofficial delegation led by the former ambassador W. W. Yen had reported that the communists had no intention of pressing their demand for the surrender of the so-called war criminals (headed by General Chiang and Madame Chiang) and were prepared to moderate the terms in other directions also. So in the third week of March an official delegation led by General Chang Chih-chun, Shao Li-tse and other leading dignitaries left for Peking, where they were received with great cordiality and entertained to banquets and receptions by Mao Tse-tung, Chou En-lai and others.

An instance of the unreal atmosphere in which the Nanking regime carried on during the first three months of 1949 when their defence had practically collapsed is provided by the following incident. General Wu Te-chen, known popularly as Wu Te, a man of great personal charm and a good record as a revolutionary general, had taken the place of Wang Shih-chieh as Foreign Minister. He summoned all the Asian Ambassadors in Nanking (Burma, Thailand, Philippines, and India) and formally proposed an alliance to fight communism everywhere. I was rather taken aback, for what he was suggesting in effect was that we should consider the Kuomintang cause as our own and make a united front with Chiang to give him support in his civil war. The Burmese Ambassador and myself opposed it strongly and the proposal was therefore still-born, but it was one of the pet ideas of Chiang Kai-shek which he tried to revive later under the joint auspices of Syngman Rhee and Quirino.

Li Tsung-jen's first difficulty was with his Cabinet. Sun Fo, the son of Sun Yat-sen, who had a vague reputation as a progressive, was the person who headed the new ministry. He and his friends decided to shift the capital to Canton, which is traditionally supposed to be the centre of Kuomintang sentiment. But the President considered that such a move would be considered by the general public as an attempt to continue the civil war. So while the Government with all the administrative offices shifted to Canton, the President and the Legislative Yuan stayed on in Nanking. The Foreign Office informed the diplomatic corps of the intended change and invited them to accompany them to Canton. They promised to make arrangements for accommodation in a hotel and to put other facilities at our disposal. On this a meeting of the diplomatic corps was convened by M. Meyrier, the French Ambassador, who was the doyen. The consensus of opinion at the meeting was that we should not accompany the Government to Canton as it was by no means certain that the Government would be able to settle down there for any length of time, and, secondly, as the President was not moving to Canton we could not legitimately leave what continued to be in theory the capital of the State. So all of us, with one notable exception—and that was the

Soviet Ambassador—sent only junior officers to represent us at Canton.

Why the Soviet Ambassador chose to leave with the Kuomintang remains a mystery. It was certainly true that the Soviets, even at this late stage, were negotiating with the Kuomintang for the renewal of the air agreement relating to Sinkiang. They were also known to have asked for agreements regarding mining concessions. It would appear from these and other reasons that the Soviets were not anticipating a quick communist victory over the "nationalists" and were ready to carry on with their legal representative at Canton accepting the Kuomintang as the legitimate Government of China.

When these discussions about the Canton move were taking place, Dr. Hu Shih called on me and had a long talk about the future. He was in a state of great nervous tension, extremely unhappy about the decision he had been forced by circumstances to take, and grieved beyond measure to see the great liberal ideas for which he had worked so hard for over thirty-five years crumbling before him. One thing which he told me then struck me very forcibly. "All this," he said, "is the fault of us liberals. When we saw how things were shaping in 1936, how the Kuomintang was renouncing the democratic idea of the Revolution and was set on the path of dictatorship and reaction, we should have protested and organized ourselves into an effective opposition. Instead we chose the easier path. Some like me left the country for the time. Others like Wang Shih-chieh joined the Government in the hope of reforming it from inside. Others remained silent and were content to carry on with their scholarly activities. If we had stood out and made ourselves heard, we could, I feel certain, have saved the liberal revolution." He talked to me much more in the same strain. I was deeply affected for I had respect not only for Hu Shih's encyclopaedic scholarship but also for his liberal idealism and for his intellectual integrity. I felt sorry that after a lifetime of work devoted to the intellectual regeneration of his country, this truly great man should at his age find himself homeless—a refugee in some foreign country. From what he told me it was clear that he had no intention of following the fortunes of Chiang Kai-shek. A professorship in some American university, well endowed with Chinese texts, seemed to be the only place where he could settle down. It was a distressing thought and it made me miserable for days, for there was no doubt that it was quite impossible for Hu Shih with his intellectual independence to adjust himself to the changed conditions.

When the Kuomintang delegates left for Peking I calculated that there would be an interval of at least three weeks during which I could go to Delhi for consultations and come back. As the communists were entrenched in force on the other bank of the Yangtse, it was a grave risk to take, especially as I was leaving my wife and children behind. If the negotiations broke down and the communists decided to attack before I returned, I would have no method of reaching them for months to come. But I calculated that, humanly speaking, it would take three weeks for the talks to break down finally and if I could return by the 20th of April, I would be in time to see the communists occupy Nanking. So I left for India and after receiving my instructions about what I should do in case the communists occupied Nanking and we were cut off from the outside world, I returned to Nanking on the 21st of April. On the 23rd the communists crossed.

On the day I was leaving for Delhi, General Li Tsung-jen invited me for dinner. He talked to me for over two hours and I had a very good opportunity of forming an estimate of his personality and the prospects of peace on the lines he was contemplating. I had of course met General Li on numerous occasions before but this was my first discussion with him after he became Acting President. Li struck me as a very well meaning, but altogether ineffective gentleman. He was hoping vaguely that the "liberal" elements in Kuomintang China would rally round him and that the United States would give him active support. His entourage consisted of a few generals of the Kwangsi clique, a few professors and journalists, who were convinced that the world could be won by statements and declarations, and his wife—a woman of remarkable beauty—whose one ambition was to outshine Madame Chiang. General Li's ideas about peace seemed to me a little naïve and unrealistic. He explained to me that he was convinced that the communists could not hope to conquer the two-thirds of China which still recognized his authority and consequently they were bound to modify their terms and accept a coalition with him. It was no doubt true that the vast area south of the Yangtse, the great provinces of Szechuan and Yunnan and outlying areas like Sikang, Kansu and Chinghai in China proper, and the immense territories of Sinkiang and Tibet were still outside communist influence. Mao Tse-tung had a much smaller area under him than the Japanese had. Li's idea was that even if the communists moved down south, he could go to Chungking from where he could defy them as Chiang defied the Japanese. "Today the position is much better," he said, "as with American help we have built aerodromes all along the interior line up to Sinkiang. There is therefore no chance of their being able to defeat us. So they are bound to jump at the offer I have made of a negotiated peace." This was his main line of argument.

Theoretically he was right. But the Japanese parallel was altogether misleading. Even in South China which he considered his stronghold, my own information showed that public opinion had swung away from the Kuomintang. Also, previous experience had demonstrated that Kuomintang soldiers were weary of fighting, and it was known that the provincial war lords were wavering. In the strategic province of Yunnan a *coup d'état* had already displaced the Kuomintang war lord, and his cousin who took over was negotiating with Mao Tse-tung. I did not of course put these doubts of mine to him, but merely asked what he thought to be the stumbling-block in the negotiations. He replied frankly that he could not agree to any conditions which would weaken the relations with America! I knew then that he was living in a fool's paradise in hoping for a negotiated settlement.

The same night I left for India. After three weeks' stay when I returned to Shanghai on the 20th of April, it became clear that I had calculated it a little too fine. Rumour was thick in Shanghai that the communists would cross the Yangtse in a day or two, and unless I left by the evening train communications between Nanking and Shanghai might be disrupted. In fact the train to

Nanking which left that night and on which I travelled was the last Kuomintang train to make the journey.

The last Kuomintang authorities had left Nanking and General Li himself was ready to leave as the news reached him that the negotiations had broken down and his own leading representatives had elected to stay in Peking. The day after I arrived (on the 22nd of April) I called on the American Ambassador, Dr. Leighton Stuart, to get from him an appraisal of the situation. Dr. Leighton Stuart was an unusual diplomat. He was a missionary educationist who had devoted over forty years of his life to the cause of Christian education for the Chinese. He had unbounded faith in Chinese character and looked upon China as his adopted home. A man of great moral rectitude and unusual simplicity of life, he was a minor Mahatma, who was perpetually surprised at the villainy of the world. His one weakness was that he was inclined to rely too much on his own judgment of Chinese character, which he idealized in some respects. As an instance he used to tell me that as the relationship of teacher and student was one of the basic conceptions of Chinese ethics, his own position as the teacher of many of the younger communist leaders would help to shape their policy in favour of the West! This naïve attitude caused him some bitter disappointments.

Dr. Leighton Stuart assured me that there was no immediate danger of the communists crossing the Yangtse and that if they attempted to do so they would lose a million men and many costly attempts would be necessary before a foothold could be established on the southern side. He added that it was also the considered opinion of the American military experts. This complacency rather astounded me, but Dr. Stuart was convinced that the defences were in perfect order and that the communists, who after all were only guerrillas, did not have the technical efficiency to carry out so elaborate a plan of ferrying across the Yangtse (not less than three quarters of a mile broad) an army of at least half a million men.

After this interview I went to see Sir Ralph Stevenson, the British Ambassador. He was more cautious, but the advice of his own experts was that the crossing of the Yangtse would not be an easy operation. "One can never know," he added however, "and the communists may be up to some tricks, but normally speaking a crossing of the Yangtse, if contested, will be a difficult operation." I had to be content with this very guarded appraisal. Half an hour after I returned home from Stevenson I got other information of a rather disquieting character. A Chinese friend told me that a citizens' committee had been formed in Nanking, headed by Dr. Wu, the celebrated President of Ginling College, to take over the maintenance of law and order in the city, and a deputation from this committee had crossed to Pukow to get in touch with the communist authorities: that it was being rumoured that the commander of the garrison of a town farther up the Yangtse had gone over to the enemy and that the communists were already crossing in force in that area; and that the local Kuomintang authorities intended quietly to slip out of the city at night.

On the 22nd of April Nanking presented a strange scene. The civil authorities having fled the town, the mob took charge. They looted systematically the houses of Kuomintang leaders and officials, but otherwise there was no hooliganism. From my chancery I could see the official residence of the mayor being plundered by the inhabitants of the locality. It was done in a civilized and orderly manner, old women being helped by younger people to carry what they had collected! The mob did not destroy anything; they broke only such things as had to be broken, like doors, window frames, etc., which some people carried away quietly as if they were withdrawing a deposit from a bank. The army headquarters, the offices of the youth organization, etc. suffered badly, but on the whole the mob behaved in an orderly and quiet manner. By the afternoon the Committee of Public Order had gained control and issued various proclamations and orders to the people.

Early next morning everyone knew that the advance party of the communists had entered Nanking and that the main force was being ferried across without any opposition. I went out into the streets to see the troops coming into Nanking. It was a strange sight. The streets were crowded with sightseers. I did not think that there was much enthusiasm, but neither was there any

D

hostility. We drove about everywhere, watching the endless procession of the P.L.A. (People's Liberation Army) marching through the famous Chung Shan Street. Except ourselves and the Burmese (and of course the Soviets) the other diplomats remained indoors, apprehensive lest their presence might lead to some untoward incidents. By the evening the crossing was completed and the Kuomintang capital effectively occupied. General Liu Po-cheng, the one-eyed dragon, as he was known, was proclaimed mayor of the city. We of the diplomatic colony were anxious and uncertain. We decided to wait on events and kept to our embassies, expecting the communists to make the first move. No such move was made; they just ignored us.

CHAPTER IV

TRAPPED IN NANKING

FOR the next three or four days there was a lull, with minor incidents which strained our nerves. A few P.L.A. soldiers had strayed into the American Embassy and walked up to the bedroom where the ambassador was lying ill with fever. They, however, left quietly after a short conversation. A few had attempted to enter the garden of the British Embassy but were dissuaded from doing so. The French, it would appear, had a bad time, for the Embassy was isolated for three days: but generally speaking, apart from the uncertainty of things, there was nothing very much for us to complain about. Provisions which had disappeared from the market became plentiful. For the time, the silver dollars of Yuan Shih-kai became the accepted currency. Everyone watched and waited.

There were two broad lines of opinion in the diplomatic body: one, which was expounded with vigour by Keith Officer, the distinguished Australian Ambassador, was that the communists would be anxious to gain the good opinion of foreign powers by treating the diplomats well. On the other hand, the Dutch Ambassador, Baron Van Arsen, produced and circulated a memorandum based on the experiences of a colleague of his in Moscow during the revolution arguing that the communists would want to be tough with us and there was no use depending on international law and usage in this matter. We did not have long to wait to find out what they intended to do. A day or two after the occupation we were politely but firmly informed that we would be given no diplomatic privileges and would be treated as only distinguished foreigners. We were alluded to as ex-ambassadors. There was no Foreign Office to deal with us, but only a Foreign Personnel Bureau where our secretaries had to present themselves with an interpreter since all business was transacted in Chinese. No communication in any other language was accepted. All conversations were in the presence of shorthand writers who took down every word that was spoken. We were not allowed the use of cypher or the privilege of using couriers. In fact we had technically ceased to be diplomatists.

We were also subjected to a number of restrictions which in the circumstances were perhaps not unreasonable. We were not allowed to go outside the city walls, even for picnics to the beautiful Lotus lake, or to the purple mountains. The reason given was that the area had not been cleared of Kuomintang bandits and the P.L.A. could not take responsibility for the lives of foreigners outside the city. The number of motor vehicles used by the embassies was strictly limited. The American Embassy had, it would seem, no less than 110 cars; it was cut down to five. The same number was allowed to Britain and France and the U.S.S.R. Italy, Holland, and Belgium were permitted three; India, Iran, etc., two: and others, one. No doubt this was necessitated by the shortage of petrol.

Apart from these inconveniences, there was no interference whatever with our life. The embassies and legations, after the minor incidents of the first few days, were left inviolate. No soldiers or policemen ever stepped into an embassy compound on any pretext whatever, and the staff and personnel were never molested, unless they broke some law in the street or elsewhere. Even the Foreign Personnel Bureau, in spite of all its tight-lipped formalism and refusal to recognize us as diplomatists, gave us in practice all the facilities we required. In one or two cases it even advanced money required for the expenditure of the mission, since exchange regulations had not come into effect. Our movements were restricted; our diplomatic activities were made impossible; but otherwise we were left to ourselves with no interference of any kind. Also, living conditions in Nanking improved after the first two weeks. Prices were stabilized and currency was steady. Life was therefore not uncomfortable.

There was, however, a nigger in the woodpile. The Chinese servants and employees, normally so docile, began suddenly to put forward impossible demands. They knew that we no longer enjoyed diplomatic privileges and in many cases they began to blackmail their employers. Dismissal for any offence became impossible, except on payment of very heavy compensation. Luggage and personal effects were distrained by servants and in one or two cases the masters were threatened with personal violence. An American officer, who was alleged to have beaten a servant, was hauled up before the Courts and had to pay a heavy fine. A motor accident leading to the injury of a Chinese led to another heavy fine. In fact the servants had the upper hand and the foreign residents, including embassy officials, were extremely nervous about the situation. Though the Chinese staff in my chancery (who were given no encouragement by the Foreign Personnel Bureau) gave us a little trouble, fortunately I was spared all worry in my own household. My No. 1 Boy, or steward, Shih, was an old-fashioned Chinese gentleman, who had been all his life in the service of diplomats. He was a staunch Buddhist, well educated and with exquisite manners. When he saw how things were shaping he came to me and told me that the communists were organizing the domestic servants of the embassies in unions and sooner or later there would be trouble with the younger men. He assured me that so far as my house was concerned he would handle it, as the other servants had been carefully selected by him. The old man was as good as his word. One day I noticed that the second boy who attended at table, etc., was absent. I asked Shih where he was. He replied with a smile that he had been replaced. I was rather troubled as I knew that replacement would mean at least six months' "severance pay" and all kinds of other worries. He guessed what was passing in my mind and hastened to add: "He went away on his own. He was sorry not to say good-bye to the master and madame. He asked to be excused." I did not say anything further then. Later on I found out that the second boy had become troublesome and threatened to take matters up to the union. Shih's reply was that as he was an army deserter he would report him as a Kuomintang vagrant and have him arrested by the communists.

The diplomatic community soon adjusted itself to the surroundings and began to organize itself in an atmosphere of insouciance.

Judge Tom Davis, the Canadian Ambassador, whom nothing worried and nothing agitated, went about tirelessly keeping up everyone's spirits. He started a bridge club for beginners and got them together every day and made them forget their worries. Tom Davis was in every way a remarkable man. He had a natural gift of friendship and he went out gaily in the firm conviction that everything was well everywhere in the world. His attitude was a fine tonic for those who were inclined to be gloomy and pessimistic. He was manfully assisted in this work by Dr. Fonseca, the Portuguese Minister, a distinguished career diplomatist who had seen service everywhere. Dr. Fonseca was a scholar and a humanist, one who viewed things with understanding. He was too complex a personality to be a perpetual optimist like Tom Davis. But theirs was a happy alliance, and the Peking-Lu Bridge Club became the standby of the more nervous among our colleagues.

Though I put in my appearance occasionally at this club, I decided to utilize this enforced holiday to more profitable purposes. I knew that we had been trapped and there was no way for us to get out till things were settled one way or the other. So I decided to divide my time into three parts, the mornings to be used for a systematic study of Chinese history and literature, the late afternoons to work on a book on the Indian Revolution, and the evenings for a translation of Kalidasa's epic the *Kumara Sambhava* into Malayalam verse. This scheme worked out fairly well. With the assistance of a professor at the Nanking university I made a collection of the serious literature on China available in English, which is indeed immense, and applied myself to it as if I were preparing for an honours school at Oxford. For my studies relating to Chinese history and literature I had also the benefit of the advice of a few American scholars who had been caught up in the same way. I liked this work greatly as it introduced me to a completely new world, to the history of Sshumma chin, to the Chronicles of the Three Kingdoms, to the social and legal theories of various Chinese schools of thought, apart from the philosophical books of Taoism. The book on the Indian Revolution (since published under the pseudonym of Chanakya) gave me an opportunity to organize my ideas on many aspects of the Indian problem. The

Indian information library was well supplied with books, and I found it especially invigorating to read the *Bhagavad Gita*, with the modern commentaries of Tilak and Aurobindo, to study carefully the writings of the Mahatma, of Vivekananda, and other makers of modern India. But the greatest pleasure was undoubtedly in the evening when I read aloud the *slokas* of *Kumara Sambhava* and tried to render them into Malayalam verse. It was a discipline more than a poetic effort. There is at least one excellent translation of *Kumara Sambhava*, the Birth of the War God, in Malayalam and there was no purpose or point in my producing an indifferent one. The discipline of translation is one which I have always appreciated, but to try one's hand at a recognized masterpiece was something which only the situation in which I was placed in China would have made me dare. The translation, though unpretentious, was I am glad to say widely welcomed when it was published three years later.

The problem of South-East Asia had always interested me. In a way my early book, *The Future of South-East Asia*, published during the war, had helped to shape policy in that area. The problem of communist expansion to the borders of Burma and Siam, which one could well foresee, began to interest me considerably. I thought the time had come to formulate a policy which would strengthen the economic, social, and political structure of the area. With this object in view I wrote a memorandum the main argument of which was that without immediate and adequate help in the economic field, the political structure of South-East Asia would provide no more than a frail barrier to the expansion of communism. I knew that my Government could not move in this matter effectively; so I decided to enlist the co-operation of the British and Australian Ambassadors and put forward the note to the Commonwealth Governments as a joint proposal. Keith Officer, the Australian Ambassador, who for all his conservatism had an imaginative mind, fell in with this idea, as did Sir Ralph Stevenson. Stevenson also showed my paper to Leighton Stuart, who it would appear agreed to recommend it independently to his Government. At the next Commonwealth Ambassadors' meeting the memorandum was approved with minor verbal modifications and it was then forwarded to our Governments as a joint proposal. A copy was also sent informally to Malcolm MacDonald, the Commissioner-General in Singapore, to enable him to discuss it at an important conference of the heads of British Missions which was due to meet in Singapore. I was told later by Keith Officer that the proposals in that memorandum formed the basis of the discussions which led to the Colombo Plan.

The diplomatic corps became more and more jittery as time went on. Apart from the fact that we had been unceremoniously deprived of our immunities and privileges, it became clear, as weeks passed by, that getting out of China was not going to be easy. Originally it was thought that once Shanghai was occupied communications with the outside world would be re-opened, and such of us as desired to go would be able to do so. Within a month of the fall of Nanking, Shanghai was also occupied, the Kuomintang as usual making but a poor show when it came to actual fighting. The western diplomats, by and large, believed that the communists would learn their lesson in Shanghai. Their favourite argument was that Shanghai had rice only for three weeks, and that the public utility services, water works, electricity, etc., depended upon imported coal, which would no longer be available. It was also fondly hoped that the spirit of Shanghai—its night clubs, its dope dens, etc.—would corrupt the communist leaders as it had corrupted the Kuomintang when the young nationalists came first into contact with the Eastern Babylon. They waited patiently for the appointed three weeks. Instead of the much-hoped-for breakdown and the pleasantly-anticipated weakening of the revolutionary spirit, the diplomatic corps in Nanking was shocked to hear the treatment meted out to an American Vice-Consul, who had been arrested and imprisoned for not obeying the orders of the military authorities. He was made to apologize and denounce his own imperialist actions. Also the prospect of leaving conveniently seemed to vanish. The Kuomintang had mined the Whampao river, and soon they proclaimed a blockade and prohibited foreign ships from entering Shanghai. The greatest port in the East lay idle. But the expected breakdown did not take place. Food was more plentiful than before. Coal for public utilities was transported from mines in the north. The communists seemed on the whole not to worry that foreign shipping was not coming to Shanghai.

To add to our discomforts, Kuomintang planes began to appear regularly over Nanking in day-time. Their object was said to be to bomb and destroy the electrically-operated ferry across the Yangtse, which carried the troop trains from the north. The power-house and the waterworks were also their targets. Though their bombing was poor and nothing of military value was ever achieved, it was sufficient to cause us intense discomfort.

My own instructions were to stay on to the last: but I knew most of the western diplomats were anxious to get out. Every day, the only topic of discussion was how to organize our departure honourably. The British Ambassador, Sir Ralph Stevenson, was in a different position. He was determined not to move from Nanking till H.M.S. *Amethyst* which had been disabled and was lying in the Yangtse moved out with or without permission. He was trying every method he knew to negotiate some kind of a settlement. As a matter affecting the honour and prestige of the Royal Navy there was considerable feeling in Britain about the incident which disabled this ship and damaged others which tried to come to her rescue. It was important that the *Amethyst* should not be left where she was. So Stevenson and his staff never talked of leaving.

The American Embassy Club, housed in the palace of the pro-Japanese President, Wang Ching Wei, had been thrown open to all the diplomatic missions. In its cool shades the diplomatic corps daily met and discussed their woes under the illusory protection of a tank, which was drawn up in front of the gate. To conceal their alarm the ladies generally played bridge but the men collected together in groups at the bar or near the swimming pool, discussed endlessly whether it was right for them to stay and whether it was not more dignified to beat a retreat. But the problem was how to leave. No ships were calling in Shanghai. It was impossible to reach Tientsin where, it was rumoured, ships were still calling. More than this, the communist authorities had resuscitated the old Chinese system of asking for two "shop guarantees" before any foreigner could leave. Shop guarantee meant that two Chinese businessmen should come forward to guarantee any continuing, contingent or future liabilities that the departing foreigner might be adjudged as being reponsible for. As we were classed as "former diplomatists" not entitled to any privileges, it was made clear that if we desired to leave, we also had to provide "shop guarantees." Our expert in international law, Baron Van Arsen, the Dutch Ambassador, searched for precedents and declared that the claim was irregular. But regular or otherwise the Chinese insisted on enforcing it. As I made up my mind to stay, till the situation cleared up, the decision did not affect me, though I agreed to join in any protest that the diplomatic corps was prepared to make. Then arose another difficulty. The communists had not claimed to be a government. They had no Foreign Office and no Ministry to which we could protest. The occupied areas were under the People's Liberation Army, and all foreigners including diplomats were dealt with by the head of the Foreign Personnel Bureau, Huang Huai. Later I came to know Huang Huai rather well when he was the official representative of the Foreign Office in Shanghai. But at this time he was not available to anyone. I dealt with him through my third secretary, Dr. Virendra Kumar, whose fluency in Chinese was of the greatest help to me at this time.

By the end of June, the patience of the diplomatic corps had practically come to an end. The summer that year was unbearably hot in Nanking and there was no way of getting out to Shanghai or to any cooler place. In the circumstances some of us decided to make an approach to the Foreign Personnel Bureau to permit us to go to Shanghai for a short visit. The permits were issued without much trouble, but we were warned that the customs authorities would insist on opening our luggage. I was, however, privately assured that the police would be instructed both in Nanking and in Shanghai to let my luggage pass without interference. That was what happened. Except for the delay in taking down the names in Chinese, we were subjected to no inconvenience, though some of the representatives of the "imperialist powers" were treated rather unceremoniously.

On the 1st of July Mao Tse-tung made the famous speech declaring firmly that new China leaned on to one side: that it aligned itself with the Soviet Union. When the speech came through we were dining at the Canadian Embassy to celebrate the Dominion National Day. The Commonwealth Ambassadors and their wives and Dr. Leighton Stuart were the only guests. One could see the effect of the speech on Dr. Leighton Stuart. That good man had hoped against hope that the communists, many of whom had been his students in Yen Ching university, would take a moderate line. But Mao Tse-tung's speech finally shattered that hope. Dr. Stuart was a broken man. He told me that he had made up his mind to leave early and had asked that his private aeroplane might be allowed to be repaired for this purpose. A few days later he left quietly and the Chinese—it must be said to their credit— gave all facilities to their old teacher to make an honourable exit. He was not harassed or troubled at the time of his departure.

The American Ambassador's departure cast a deep gloom over the foreign colony. It was clear that the present position was untenable. The French Ambassador decided to ask for an evacuation ship to be sent from Indo-China, but it was not easy to make the necessary arrangements for leaving the country. Also the American Government were sending up a ship—the *Gordon Castle*, I think it was called—to enable the large American colony in Shanghai and the diplomatic personnel to return home. But the British, on whom the rest of us were depending for evacuation, still made no move. This seemed rather alarming to others but it was quite clear that as ample shipping facilities existed in Hong Kong, Britain could at a moment's notice make arrangements without any fuss. She was waiting for something to happen in the *Amethyst* case.

And indeed something did happen. Quietly one night the *Amethyst* steamed out and braving the communist guns escaped into the high seas. It was a notable feat, in the best traditions of the Royal Navy. The full story of its escape has not been disclosed. But when it is told it will, I am sure, be one of high adventure, gallantry and courage. The *Amethyst* had been heavily damaged, and as no one was allowed on board the possibility of adequate repairs being effected on the boat seemed very remote. The communists were very vigilant and kept constant watch. Besides even if at dead of night it could have moved away silently under the cover of Chinese junks going up and down the river, the stretch of Yangtse from Nanking to the sea was too long for it to escape without notice. But escape it did, and the feeling in Britain was as if a new battle of Trafalgar had been won.

The British Embassy breathed freely again and Sir Ralph Stevenson began occasionally to discuss the problem of our return. He did not want to leave too early and give the impression of deserting his post, nor did he want to stay once the position had become definitely irregular. We were, in general terms, aware of what was happening in Peking. The communist leaders had convened a conference of all parties there and they were discussing a common programme on the basis of which the new Government of China was going to be proclaimed. It was known that General Li Chi-shen, leader of the Kuomintang Revolutionaries, Chang Lan, the leader of the Democratic League, Huang Wen-pai, the radical leader, besides non-party personages like Madame Sun Yat-sen and Kuo Mo-jo, the historian and writer, were co-operating with the communists in working out the principles of a coalition and a programme of political action. I was very definite that once a Government was officially proclaimed, the diplomatic representatives could not stay on without recognizing that Government. I kept on pressing this point of view and affirming that the only right we possessed, once such a Government was established, was the right of exit. In this point of view I was supported by Mr. Finaltea, the Italian Ambassador on whose family the strain had begun to tell. Another diplomat who was also in favour of joint action for withdrawal immediately the Government was proclaimed was Le Ghait, the Belgian Ambassador, whose previous experience in Moscow and generally detached and philosophical attitude was appreciated by all. Le Ghait was a scholar. As he was then a bachelor he had plenty of time to devote to his studies, which included at that time, I do not know how seriously, Chinese grammar!

As most of us anticipated, the Central Government of the People's Republic of China was proclaimed from the square of the Tien An-men or the Gate of Heavenly Peace, on the 1st of October, 1949. Mao Tse-tung was of course Chairman. Among the Vice-Chairmen appeared the names of Madame Sun Yat-sen, Chang Lan, and General Li Chi-shen. It was significant of the state of our knowledge on China that even professed experts on Chinese communism did not know whether Kao Kang was a communist or democratic leader. Not one of the diplomatists in Nanking, including those who had the most widespread intelligence services, had heard of Kao Kang. As for Liu Shao-chi, only those of us who had been trying to follow the theoretical writings of Chinese communism knew that he was a very important person. Chou En-lai was Prime Minister and Foreign Minister, and the first thing he did on the proclamation of the People's Republic was to summon the foreign representatives in Peking and hand over to them a communication inviting the establishment of diplomatic relations. Letters addressed by name were sent to the head of the Foreign Personnel Bureau at Nanking, Huang Huai, to be handed over to the representatives of powers stationed there. The next day Huang Huai summoned the heads of Missions (those who had no Consuls in Peking) to his office. Most of them agreed to go, but I sent word that if Mr. Chou En-lai had sent a communication to me it might be sent on to my residence, and that I would not personally attend at the Bureau at Huang's call. The Foreign Personnel Bureau received my reply very well and suggested that I might send a secretary to receive the communication. I sent Dr. Kumar, my third secretary, and the communication was handed over to him. My interim reply, promising to forward the communication to Delhi and addressed to "General Chou En-lai, Peking," was sent the same day to Mr. Huang for transmission to Peking. Prime Minister Nehru's reply, which arrived two days later, was couched in very friendly terms, indicating that there would be early recognition and exchange of representatives.

The question of withdrawal had thus become an immediate one. Delhi was anxious that I should stay on in Nanking but I pointed out that while I was prepared to stay on I would have no official position and could not carry on any work till the regime was officially recognized. Recognition was bound to take time as the Kuomintang was still in occupation not only of Canton, but of vast areas in the south-east, including Szechuan, Yunnan, and Sikang, and the civil war was unlikely to end on the mainland for another two or three months. On my representing this the Prime Minister agreed to my withdrawing with the other diplomatists.

The arrangements for withdrawal were in British hands. They arranged for two boats, one belonging to Butterfield and Swire and the other to Jardin Mathesons, and accommodation was provided for all the diplomatic staff who desired to use British good offices. Besides the British ships, the French and the Americans had also requisitioned boats for their nationals and friends. Most of the European and Asian representatives preferred however to go by the British ships.

One major issue which worried everyone but about which very little was spoken was in respect of our treatment by the Customs officials. A. K. Sen, who had been carrying on the work of the Consul-General in Shanghai, had succeeded in establishing fairly friendly relations with the Foreign Bureau there, and he assured me that so far as our luggage was concerned there would be no difficulty and that it would be allowed to go through without examination. He said that he believed the same courtesy would be shown to the Burmese also. And it actually happened that way. But their treatment of European diplomats varied. The British and Australian Ambassadors' luggage was opened only formally— just to emphasize the right. In some other cases they searched the packages carefully, in every case insisting that they did not recognize any diplomatic privileges for "former diplomatists."

Anyway, it could not be described as an honourable exit and most of the diplomats regretted that they had stayed behind at all. They had hoped that the communists would appreciate the fact that they had not followed the Kuomintang Government in its wanderings on the mainland; that the communist authorities would interpret their stay as a demonstration of practical sympathy. It did not take many weeks before disillusionment came. The Chinese communists were not standing any patronage from the West: and it was as sadder and wiser men that most of them embarked on British ships, which evacuated the last survival of imperialist domination from the mainland of China.

CHAPTER V

AN INTERLUDE IN INDIA

WE reached Hong Kong after a few days. The Governor of Hong Kong, Sir Alexander Grantham, was a senior officer of the Colonial service whom I had met before in Lagos where he had been Chief Secretary. He was an administrator of exceptional ability and political understanding and it was lucky for Hong Kong that its affairs were under his charge. This little islet, separated from the mainland only by a narrow stretch of water, had become the haven of refugees both from the Kuomintang and from the communists. Its population had, at all times, been predominantly Chinese, and the colony depended for its economic life on trade with the mainland. During the days of Kuomintang authority the opposition had always found it convenient to retire to Hong Kong, after the foreign concessions had ceased to exist. Thus, the Revolutionary Committee of the Kuomintang, under General Li Chi-shen, had made the colony its headquarters. The communists also had maintained an office there for contacting the outside world and this office was run by Chiao Kan-hua, then known as Cho Mu, and his talented wife.

When the communist victory in the battle of Hsuchow made it clear that the power of the Kuomintang was broken and it was only a question of time for the People's Liberation Army to take over the south, the rich compradores, the millionaire businessmen, and others who felt that life might not be easy for them in New China hurried to Hong Kong. Among the dignitaries who had thus found refuge were the notorious Tu Yeh-shen, Sun Fo, the son of Sun Yat-sen, and the last Kuomintang premier in Nanking, Yen Hsi-shan the war lord of Shensi who had maintained his independence of the Kuomintang to the very last, and numerous other less well-known officials. It was said of Yen Hsi-shan that he had long ago foreseen the possibility of exile and had built for himself a magnificent palace and five other bungalows for his five concubines. Actually the population of the island had more than doubled during the few months preceding our arrival and it was overcrowded to a degree which was unbelievable. But though the administration was a little nervous of the intentions of the communists, and was fully aware that the island could not be defended against a major attack, life went on normally. One could feel the tension in the air, and that was natural, but the Governor and his staff were fully satisfied that a military crisis was not likely to develop. There might be grave internal problems, strikes, a projection of the Kuomintang-communist strife among the Chinese population, etc. These they were prepared to deal with.

Hong Kong has an old established and prosperous Indian population numbering no less than three thousand. Some of the families, like the Ruttonjees, were as old as the colony itself, having been established there even before the British formally acquired it by the Treaty of Nanking. All Indian business communities were well represented, Gujaratis, Parsis, Sindhis and even one or two people from Malabar. The Sindhi houses were among the most adventurous in the Far East. The Indian merchants were mainly in the export and import trade and had during the last hundred years contributed much to the prosperity of the colony. The Ruttonjee family endowed munificently a tuberculosis hospital among other charitable institutions. I was glad to note that these hard-headed businessmen were not in any way alarmed by the changes on the mainland. Mr. Ruttonjee had in fact begun the construction of a villa in Stanley overlooking the main coast.

I was anxious to see conditions in Burma a little before reaching India. The civil war was then at its height. Everyone knew that the writ of the Central Government did not run far beyond Rangoon itself. The Karens, and numerous leftist factions fighting the Government, seemed for the time to have the upper hand. As I anticipated that the Chinese communists would reach the Burmese borders in two or three months' time, I was anxious to judge for myself the chances of survival of the U Nu Government. We were received with great cordiality in Rangoon and we had through the kindness of Mr. Rauf, our Ambassador, an opportunity of

E

discussing matters with the leading personalities. Though in Rangoon itself there was ample evidence of military precautions against a surprise attack, and the public generally felt that life had its dangers, the leaders of Government seemed very optimistic. U Nu had just then formulated his one-year plan of peace and was vigorously canvassing support for his ideas in the country-side. The general opinion was that the communist threat was no more than a nuisance and the danger to the State was from the rebellion of the Karens. The claim of the Karens threatened to disrupt the State and it was clear that the Burmese Government was right in giving priority to the defeat of the disruptionists. The general feeling was that the strength of the Government was growing, that the army which was being organized and trained was making itself felt, and that in a few months the situation would improve from the economic and political point of view.

The Indian Ambassador in Rangoon, Rauf, was in many ways a remarkable man. He was born in Burma and was a leader of the Rangoon Bar. Before India's independence he was a political figure of some consequence in Burma and had been a close associate of the present ministers many of whom he had known from their early days. His brother Rashid is married to a Burmese lady and is now a minister in the Burmese Government after having opted for and acquired Burmese nationality. Naturally, Rauf was in a position to know from the inside what was happening in the country and to form an unbiased conclusion. His own view was that U Nu was gaining both in stature and in authority, and, accidents and unforeseen events apart, he would be able to pull the country through.

We had some old friends in Burma, notably a young woman of brilliant abilities, Daw Mimi-khiang, the wife of a minor Shan prince who was in charge of education in the Shan area. During the war Mimi-khiang was in India and had come and stayed with us in Bikaner. She was a person of sound and independent judgment and from her also I was able to confirm the conclusions which I had formed as a result of my talks with the Ambassador and the leaders of Government. Thus after a short but profitable stay we returned to India by the beginning of November.

The Prime Minister's intention was to send me back to China. I knew that some of the chief permanent officials in the Foreign Office were opposed to this, on the ground that it would be against protocol to send up my name in view of the fact that I had already been Ambassador to the Kuomintang regime. It was clear, however, that the Peking Government attached no importance to this consideration, as they had already welcomed General N. V. Roschin, our colleague in Nanking, as Soviet Ambassador to the new regime. But I had to wait in India till the Government decided to announce their recognition and to establish diplomatic relations with Peking.

While there was no difference of opinion as to the necessity of recognizing the new China, there was a difference of opinion among the leaders about its timing. The more conservative members of the Congress leadership, including C. Rajagopalachari who was then the Governor-General and Sardar Vallabhai Patel, wanted us to go slow in the matter. They were supported in this attitude by a powerful section of the Civil Service, including, I suspect, some of the senior officials of the Foreign Office. My own view to which I gave free expression was that we should recognize the new regime when the Kuomintang authority on the mainland of China ceased to function. Chiang Kai-shek's fugitive regime was then in Chungking. Many people believed that, as at the time of the Japanese war, the Kuomintang would be able to hold out in this inaccessible area. The American doctrine at that time was that if the Kuomintang could control Yunnan, Szechuan, Sikang, and the outer provinces, covering what was generally claimed to be the areas controlled by the Muslim war lords which extended to Sinkiang and the Soviet border, then American strategic requirements would be satisfied. Large aerodromes had been constructed in this interior line during the anti-Japanese war, and some American military leaders had assured me that with bases in Indo-China and Siam this line could be effectively defended and converted into a vital area for American "defence" purposes. It is not so ridiculous a scheme as it sounds now. If American policy had been definite and firm and the State Department had been ready to intervene even indirectly as General

Chenault and others desired, the Kuomintang Government could have been propped up for a time and at least the outer provinces might have been detached and organized into a separate state. But that would have meant intervention in civil war. That was what Chiang and his friends were hoping for. However, at this crucial period, American policy was indecisive. A controversy had broken out in the U.S.A. as to who was responsible for the failure of America's Chinese policy, and the State Department hit back by publishing the famous White Paper, which was a most damaging analysis of Kuomintang policies and actions. The result of this internal squabble was political vacillation and consequently at this critical time America had no policy in regard to China. It was well known that the State Department was discussing with the British Government the question of recognition and, though no decision was taken, the general impression was that America at this stage was not unfavourable to the idea of other powers recognizing China. Perhaps it was even prepared to consider doing so itself. A significant indication of how widespread this attitude was is provided in Foster Dulles' own volume *War or Peace* where he frankly states that recognition of Peking China might be necessary.

The agitation of a few Republican leaders, popularly associated with the China Lobby, had not had much effect at this time (November–December, 1949) and it was clear that without active American support the Kuomintang regime at Chungking could not hold out. The decision that Mr. Nehru took was therefore to convey our recognition when the Kuomintang Government moved into the island of Formosa, which at the time was still juridically a part of the Japanese Empire since the treaty transferring it to the Allies had not been signed. Britain also agreed with this view and it was decided that the Indian Government's recognition of the new Government of China should be conveyed to Peking by the end of the year. For some reason Burma was anxious that it should be the first State outside the Soviet *bloc* to recognize the New China and we were approached with a request to wait for a few days in order to give Burma the start. In due course, Burma announced its recognition and we followed in a few days. Britain, Pakistan, and Indonesia also announced their recognition: so by the first week of January, 1950, the Peking Government had received the recognition of the major Asian States.

Peking's reaction was rather unexpected. As a preliminary step it suggested that envoys should be sent to Peking to discuss the details of the exchange of diplomatic representatives. As A. K. Sen, who was my first secretary in Nanking, was still there, he was asked as chargé d'affaires to go up to Peking and discuss matters. We, as well as the other nations including Britain, had assumed that diplomatic relations would automatically follow recognition of the new Government, and that the previous embassies would therefore be automatically revived without discussion or argument. That, however, was not the Chinese point of view. They held that diplomatic relations had to be settled separately by negotiations. Rather hastily, the recognizing powers agreed to send their representatives to Peking. Looking back on it, it would clearly have been more advantageous to ask the power which requested recognition to send its representative, or, as is normal in such circumstances, to take up the negotiations in neutral capitals where both parties were represented. Proceeding on the assumption that recognition involved the re-establishment of diplomatic relations, the Government of India had nominated Sen as chargé d'affaires. Peking refused to accept this and we in our turn refused to carry on the talks unless he was so recognized. Sen was asked to put a specific question as to whether the Chinese negotiators recognized him as chargé. If the answer was in the negative he was instructed to withdraw from the talks. On this, the Chinese compromised and replied that they recognized him as chargé d'affaires for this purpose. After this preliminary exchange the negotiations were easy, but the formal announcements took a little time, as both Mao Tse-tung and Chou En-lai were away in Moscow discussing the Sino-Soviet treaty. As soon as the establishment of diplomatic relations was announced, Sen took over as proper chargé d'affaires. Soon afterwards the Chinese Government also communicated their agreement to my nomination to the post.

I had been in India for about five months and during this

period I had been nominated temporarily to the Public Service Commission, primarily to represent the External Affairs Ministry. The Commission interviewed candidates in Delhi, Allahabad, Patna, Calcutta, Madras, Nagpur and Bombay. For many years I had been out of touch with the younger generation and this all-India tour, extending over four months, gave me an exceptional opportunity of judging both the quality of our university education and the intellectual capacities of the new generation. It was an interesting experience. What struck me most was the absence of an all-India mind among the young men, the result mainly of the provincialization of the universities following the Montagu-Chelmsford Reforms (1921). Another thing that struck me was that while most of the candidates for the administrative or foreign services had a fair knowledge of European history, they were, by and large, ignorant of the historical background of Asian countries. What little they knew was from the British point of view. This was not the fault of the students or even of the universities. There were no books on the modern history of Asian countries written from the Asian point of view. This was so glaring a fact even in regard to India, that I had been approached a few months after the interim Government was established to write a one-volume history of India for Indians: in fact to make an attempt to restore the perspective of Indian history. The only book which had done this to some extent was Nehru's own *Discovery of India*, which, though sound history, was more of a literary work. I undertook to do this and the result was a *Survey of Indian History* published in August, 1947. It was now suggested to me by R. N. Bannerji, the Chairman of the Public Services Commission, that I should write a survey of modern Asian history from the point of view of Asians themselves. The idea of writing a history of European relations with Asia had attracted me for a long time and Bannerji's suggestion thus accorded with my own plans. As, later, in China I had ample time at my disposal, and the advantages of being able to use the excellent National Library and the library of the Peking University, I was able to fulfil this promise and publish (in 1953) my *Asia and Western Dominance*.

When we were waiting for a reply from Peking about my nomination, the Indo-Pakistan relations had reached a sudden and unprecedented crisis. This time the centre of trouble was not the Punjab but Bengal. Arising out of some minor incident, the attitude of the Government and the Muslim majority in East Pakistan became suddenly unfriendly. The result was an unprecedented exodus of Hindus from Bengal, bringing with them the familiar and no doubt exaggerated stories of forced conversions, loot, etc. The repercussions on the Indian side were equally disastrous. After a few days, Muslims from West Bengal began a panicky flight into Pakistan. We were back in the dark days of 1947. Though there was not the same massacre of the innocents, this time the crisis was more serious in so far as leaders on both sides had begun to talk of war. When the crisis was at its height I was asked whether I would go as High Commissioner to Pakistan and handle the situation. I looked upon it as a challenge and unhesitatingly agreed to do so. But before the matter could be finally arranged the reply from China arrived agreeing to my nomination as Ambassador to Peking. Also, in a day or two the Indo-Pakistan situation took a sudden turn for the better as a result of the direct contact established between the two Prime Ministers. So the original proposal of my going to Peking was allowed to stand.

At the end of April I left for Peking. After a two days' stay in Hong Kong where the Press was most intrigued about my assignment, we embarked for Tientsin on the Butterfield and Swire ship, the *Poyang*.

The *Poyang* was a coaster of no more than 3,000 tons and as it carried very little cargo—a mere forty tons—it pitched and rolled when there was even the suspicion of a breeze. One day, half-way up to Tientsin, a nationalist gunboat was sighted but it went past us. The gunboat did not frighten us so much as the elaborate precautions taken by the company against the possibility of an attack by pirates. At every important point on the ship, guards armed with rifles were posted who watched the ship day and night. They wore on their shoulders the legend A.P.G. (anti-pirate guards). The rails separating the aft of the ship, occupied by

Chinese deck passengers, had frightening spikes, and the movements of these passengers were carefully watched all the time.
This gave our voyage the appearance of a perilous adventure. I
enquired of one of the officers why all this precaution was being
taken. His reply was that the danger from piracy was a real one
and when a boat carried Chinese deck passengers there was no
certainty that at least a few of them were not disguised pirates,
ready to overwhelm the crew and take control of the ship at any
time. He mentioned to me a few recent instances, one of which
related to quite a large liner ! The *Poyang* had on board a number
of Chinese deck passengers, and after hearing all the stories about
pirates I often used to stand at the barrier and try to scrutinize the
faces of these men, wondering if I could spot a pirate !

I recall very well the feelings which agitated me as the boat
entered the Taku Bar. I knew I was entering a strange and new
world. I knew that my previous experience, either in the West or
in Kuomintang China, would be of no great help to me. My
knowledge of communism was only from books. In fact, except
for the Soviet and Eastern *bloc* diplomats in Nanking, I had not
known any communists at all. All my training has been in the
liberal radicalism of the West and consequently, though I was in
some measure familiar with the economic doctrines of Marx, I
had no sympathy for a political system in which individual liberty
did not find a prominent place. But as against all this, I had a deep
feeling of sympathy for the Chinese people, a desire to see them
united, strong and powerful, able to stand up against the nations
which had oppressed them for a hundred years, a psychological
appreciation of their desire to wipe out the humiliations which
followed the western domination of their country and to proclaim
the message of Asia Resurgent. In these matters the attitudes of
India and China were similar. Where they differed was in their
political structure, in their conception of social life, and perhaps
more than even that, in their attitude to the world. India had taken
up openly the position that the world could not be divided into
sheep and goats: that the idea that there can be only two camps in
the world, the Faithful and the Kafir, was basically unsound. Mao
Tse-tung, on the other hand, had publicly proclaimed his faith that

there can be only two camps and all who are not of the Faithful are Kafirs. It was my mission, as I saw it, to prove it to him that a neutral position was also possible.

I looked upon my forthcoming assignment with much curiosity but with no sense of depression. I knew it would not be any easy life. I knew there were issues on which India and China were likely to disagree, but I felt that, given a reasonable opportunity, I might be able to establish a basis of relationship which would work out advantageously to both countries.

CHAPTER VI

ARRIVAL IN COMMUNIST PEKING

IT was on the 13th of May (1950) that I arrived at Tientsin. The journey from Hong Kong had seemed interminably long though it only took seven days. The captain of the ship, a Scotsman named Holmes, had many stories about the communists in Shanghai and Tientsin. On the whole his impression seemed to be that the new regime was efficient and meant business. He also informed me that the Americans seemed to be doing good business in Tientsin and that two U.S. ships had lately brought raw cotton for the Tientsin mills and had returned fully loaded. I mention this only to show that the fanatical attitude towards China, which the American public was slowly developing, had not yet reached the stage where it interfered with free enterprise.

We weighed anchor at about 2.30 in the afternoon. The re-entry into China was indeed different from the departure only a few months ago. Then we had left without ceremony. There was no one to see us off. We were "ex-ambassadors" going away unhonoured because we were not wanted. Everything, including exit permits, had to be asked for as a favour. Now the position was totally different. The vice-mayor on behalf of the city administration, and the Chief of Protocol in Tientsin on behalf of the Foreign Office, came on board with the Indian chargé d'affaires, Sen, to welcome me. The vice-mayor even made a short speech! We stayed for the day at the Astoria House Hotel.

Tientsin, like Shanghai, had been a foreign city, divided into British, French, and other concessions. The houses are in foreign style and the streets have a European appearance. I liked Tientsin better than Shanghai, though it is less pretentious and does not boast of skyscrapers, clubs with unusually long bars, and the other specialities of the Paris of the East. Tientsin seemed to me better spread out, more solid, and less artificial than Shanghai. After the war, as a result of the exclusion of the Japanese, German, and Italian business, the economic life of the city came to be dominated by the three British business giants, Butterfield and Swire, Jardin Mathesons, and the Kailan Mining Administration, nominally a Sino-British corporation but in fact a British one. With the coming of the communists, however, the position of the foreign business community had been made extremely difficult. The Tientsin Tug and Lighter Company which is a Butterfield and Swire concern, for example, had not been allowed to operate, as the river had been declared an inland waterway; yet it had to pay all its Chinese staff. The Kailan Mines Administration, which is one of the biggest investments in the East, was, it was reported, on the point of bankruptcy though its daily extraction of coal amounted then to 14,000 tons. Other foreign concerns were no better off.

We left for Peking the next day. A large special carriage had been reserved for my party and I was accompanied by an English-speaking officer of the Protocol who supplied us every few minutes with fresh cups of tea. An interesting fact about the journey was that all the attendants in the train were women. I was informed that even in such "men's work" as driving locomotives women were now being freely employed. Ma Mu-ming—the protocol officer—also told me, and I had the statement verified later, that an express train from Manchuria had been brought into Peking staffed exclusively by women. Certainly in New China women seemed to have come into their own.

The train arrived in Peking punctually at 6.30. I was, however, asked to wait inside the carriage for a minute to be officially welcomed by the authorities. A minute later Wang Ping-nan, head of the general office of the Ministry of Foreign Affairs, Wang Jo-ju, Chief of Protocol, Wu Han, vice-mayor of Peking, and other dignitaries came into the carriage and expressed their welcome in a short speech in Chinese, which was, of course, translated to me. I naturally replied in English. After this exchange of compliments I was escorted outside and presented to the representatives of other missions who had come there to receive me. All the foreign missions including the Soviet Mission were represented by senior officials. General Rochin, the Soviet Ambassador, had even sent a special message of welcome through his counsellor. From the station I was taken to the Wagon-Lit Hotel.

The Wagons-lit is one of the most famous hostelries in the East; often alluded to with a sense of glamour and romance in the literature relating to China. Like Shepheard's Hotel in Cairo, it was also associated with diplomats and other international personages. Situated in the heart of what was the Legation Quarter, that Mecca of racialism with the great embassies of England, France, U.S.A., Japan, Russia, and Germany surrounding it, the Grand Hôtel des Wagons-lit once symbolized the dominance which the European nations had established in the imperial city itself. The Legation Quarter was an enclave, acknowledging no authority of the former Chinese Government, fortified, policed and defended by the powers, who had barracks attached to the legations in which foreign troops were quartered. Under the terms of the Boxer protocol, the powers had even reserved the right of excluding the Chinese from this area.

In its general layout, in the architectural style of its buildings, and in general atmosphere the Legation Quarter was a bit of Europe transplanted into China. The legations—elevated to embassies during the latter days of the Kuomintang—were truly fantastic. The British Embassy covers an enormous area, enclosed by a high wall, in which the central place is occupied by a Chinese pavilion. The embassy house, constructed on the model of a British country residence, was no doubt meant to impress the "Heathen Chinese." The other European nations, and of course Japan, had followed the lead of the British. The great powers vied with each other and the lesser ones like Belgium and Holland tried within their means to live up to the standards set by the great powers.

The Grand Hôtel des Wagons-lit had been a kind of miniature expression of this spirit. When I visited Peking in September, 1948, almost at the very end of the Kuomintang period, there was still a faint reflection of its past glory. The bar was crowded at all times and the lounge was noisy and gay with crowds of American men and women and a sprinkling of Europeans of all nationalities. It had then the atmosphere of a continental hotel frequented by American tourists. The most flourishing trade inside the hotel was then in curios, mostly fakes, which were bought at fabulous prices by foreigners. All transactions then were in dollars and those who did not have a plentiful supply of that currency felt practically left out.

Now of course the situation was entirely changed. A week or two before I arrived, the hotel had been acquired from its British proprietors by the People's Government to be used for official purposes. The curio shops had received notice to quit and there was neither noise nor gaiety in the lounge. The hotel was, however, full, not only with the members of foreign missions waiting to find accommodation, but with a large group of Soviet technicians who were occupying two whole floors. After two or three weeks, it ceased to be a hotel and was turned over to the Soviet experts as a hostel.

Of course, the Legation Quarter is now called by that name only by foreigners. During the Japanese occupation its privileges had more or less ceased. When the Kuomintang took over Peking after the war, the European nations had given up extra-territoriality and with it the immunities and franchises they had enjoyed in the Legation Quarter. When the People's Government was formally established, it proceeded to evict the British, the French, and the Americans from lands which they had 'illegally' encroached upon to build barracks. With that, the last symbol of the special position of the Legation Quarter also vanished.

I had made up my mind from the beginning to select a residence for myself outside the Legation area. I had no desire to be associated with the Quarter, which stood so much for European domination in the East. The house which Sen, in consultation with the Foreign Office, had selected for me, was one facing the city wall on a main street between the Cheng Men and Ho Ping Men. The house belonged to some Chinese dignitary, who apart from numerous courtyards and houses and reception rooms in Chinese style had also built for his own convenience a modern house with up-to-date fittings. In the front of this house which was situated away from the street was a beautiful rock-garden and a number of old and noble trees. The pavilion attached to the garden had scenes from the *Dream of the Red Chamber* painted on its sides. The house was in keeping with the atmosphere of the city and had also the conveniences of a modern building.

Three days after my arrival, Chou En-lai, the Prime Minister, received me in the main drawing room at the Wai Chiaopu—the Chinese Foreign Office. Like everyone else interested in Far Eastern politics I had not only heard of Chou but had followed his career from the days when he was Deputy Commander of the Shanghai rebellion, which is the theme of Malraux' *Condition Humaine*. I was, therefore, looking forward to the interview. After I had been shown into the drawing-room Chou walked in. He is a well-set-up, handsome man, youthful in appearance, with a mass of black hair and a face which is pleasant and at the same time completely composed. He was dressed in the standard black closed coat and trousers with the inevitable fountain-pen sticking out from the pocket. He walked into the room with calm dignity and accosted me with cordiality. We settled down for a long talk.

Considering that Chou En-lai had perhaps the most difficult job in the world—as he was both the Prime Minister and Foreign Minister of China, besides being one of the Vice-Chairmen of the Supreme Military Council, and a member of the central executive committee of the Party—he appeared to me to possess an extraordinary serenity of countenance. Nehru, whom he resembles in many respects, looks worried, except when he smiles or laughs in company. Chou En-lai smiles only faintly and he generally maintains an attitude of impenetrability. What I noticed first about him were his hands. Not only were they carefully tended, but the fingers were like tender onion shoots, as the Chinese describe them, and he gesticulated with them with great effect.

Our conversation lasted for exactly an hour and a half. His questions to me were most penetrating and dealt mainly with problems of industrial production, land owning, conditions of the peasantry, etc. His information about India seemed to be vague, and all his questions touched on issues which were common to India and China. I felt he was making comparisons all the time in order to understand the differences and similarities of our problems. He came back again and again to the question of steel and electric power and during the talk told me how important it was for Asian peoples that our capacity in these two fields should be increased.

After this long interview, which ended as usual with toasts, I came away with the impression that I was talking with one who was no doctrinaire, but a practical statesman, one with whom it was possible to discuss and do business. Clearly, he was fully aware of the realities behind and beyond politics. Chou En-lai is, without doubt, a staunch and convinced communist and a trained theoretician but he also has his feet firmly planted on mother earth.

The next day the Chief of Protocol called on me at the hotel to inform me that the Chairman (Mao Tse-tung) had fixed 5 p.m. on the 20th for the presentation of my Letters of Credence. I was, in a measure, relieved, as I had heard that the Rumanian and Czech Ambassadors had presented their credentials at eleven o'clock at night, as Mao Tse-tung had no other time to spare. In fact one of the curious things in China which I noticed later was the tendency of the new regime to have their interviews late at night, perhaps as a result of conferences and discussions which went on interminably during day time. At least three of my important interviews with Chou En-lai took place after 10 p.m. and one very important interview was at midnight!

I confess I was not a little excited at the idea of a talk with one who had changed the course of history so violently in Asia. Was he a new Chingiz, an emperor thinking in terms of altering the map of a continent, or the chosen leader of a resurgent people, driving out those who had sold out the Chinese Revolution and pushing back to the sea, from whence they came, the western nations who had enslaved the nations of Asia? How did he, this rough-hewn warrior bred on mountain-tops and in caves, compare with Mahatma Gandhi and Nehru, the liberators of the 350 millions of India, and with his old enemy, Chiang Kai-shek? I had read that he was a student of classical Chinese literature. It was clear that he was a thinker of originality, for his published writings on *New Democracy, On a Coalition Government,* etc., showed a powerful and analytical mind.

The presentation of credentials took place with the usual ceremonies in the Chairman's official residence, one of the smaller palaces of the Manchu emperors situated on the shores of the south lake. It was said to have been built by the Emperor Chien Lung for his Turki favourite, known as the Fragrant Concubine. The entrance to the palace is through a gate, where once stood, it is said, a tower from which the Fragrant Lady used to show herself to her relatives, a very exceptional favour according to the court etiquette which governed the harem of the Son of Heaven. Mao Tse-tung did not live in this palace. He resided with his wife, a very good-looking woman, who is reputed to have been a cinema actress, in the Hunting Lodge in the summer hills. The formal ceremony was short and impressive and while I emphasized in my speech how the cause of peace would be strengthened by a policy of firm friendship between India and China, Mao Tse-tung in his turn alluded not only to our common traditions but also to our common struggles to recover our freedom.

After the ceremony was over Mao Tse-tung led me to a small reception room where we talked about India and China for over half an hour. Only Chou En-lai and an interpreter were present, besides ourselves. Mao opened the conversation by saying that in China there was an old belief that if a man lived a good life he would be reborn in India. We talked about Asia in general and about the withdrawal of Europeans from the continent, but he said more than once that as long as European economic power was entrenched in Asia the freedom was not complete. My reply was that the right method of excluding European economic power was by the development of our own resources and that we in India were determined to follow this policy. He also asked me about conditions in Burma and seemed greatly interested when I told him that the Burmese Government was as determined as we were to maintain their full independence. He showed considerable interest in Buddhism and asked what influence it had in India. Another question in which he seemed interested was the nature of our relations with Britain. The conversation was extremely cordial and again many toasts were drunk to the friendship between our two countries.

Mao Tse-tung is a little over average height: in fact for a southerner he may be considered a tall man. He is heavily built, with broad shoulders and short but thick neck. The impression which his face conveys is pleasant and benevolent and the look in his eyes is kindly. His forehead is broad and the encroaching baldness makes it even more impressive. The mass of black hair that crowns his head frames the face effectively. His personality is impressive but not intimidating and he has the gift of making people feel at home. There is no cruelty or hardness either in his eyes or in the expression of his mouth. In fact he gave me the impression of a philosophical mind, a little dreamy but absolutely sure of itself. From his early days in his father's little farm to his present dazzling eminence the way had been hard and long. In the hills of Ching Kan-shan, resisting the punitive expeditions of Chiang, leading his flock like a new Moses to the promised land in an unparalleled trek across mountains, ridges, and deserts, living in caves in Yenan, fighting the K.M.T., which was determined on annihilating him, organizing guerrillas against the Japanese, and finally planning the great war of reconquest which gave to him mastery over the whole of China, from Manchuria to the borders of India and Indo-China, over a territory such as no Chinese ruler since Kangsi had controlled, Mao Tse-tung in his epic life must have experienced many hardships and endured tremendous sufferings. Yet his face showed no signs of bitterness, cruelty or sorrow.

Mao Tse-tung speaks with a soft voice and his speech is not hurried. He has a sense of history which came out in many ways during our conversation. For example, he wanted to know the relationship of the great Moguls to the Mongols. He also felt deeply as an historical thinker the injustices that European imperialism had inflicted on Asia. It seemed to be his view that Europe had unbalanced the life in Asia, and the work of this generation of liberators was to recover the balance.

For one who was nearing sixty and had undergone the troubles he had to go through Mao seemed healthy and vigorous. The

F

peasant stock from which he comes is probably the hardiest in the world, and Mao, in spite of his worries as the head of a great State and probably the most hard-worked man in China, seemed well able to stand it.

To compare Mao with Chiang Kai-shek would be unfair. Chiang is no doubt a forceful personality, a man of determination and character, but he was hard and self-centred with a streak of cruelty in him. The way he rooted out the family of General Yang for three generations, including the youngest children, for the crime of having detained him in Sian is indicative of his revengeful spirit. Also, it had never been claimed for him that Chiang was a man of culture. A more profitable comparison would be with Nehru. Both are men of action, but with dreamy, idealistic temperaments. While both may be considered humanists in the broadest sense of the term, Nehru has his roots in Western liberalism which affects even his socialist thinking. Mao Tse-tung, being mostly self-educated, with his economics and history learnt from Marx and Lenin, has perhaps no use for the liberal creed of individual liberty. However, as one bred in the classical literature of China, with an early Buddhist training, it is perhaps fair to add that Mao has something more than the dry theories of Marxism in his mental make-up.

The next few days were taken up by visits to leading Chinese personalities. In turn I called on Chu Teh, Liu Shao-chi, Li Chi-shen, Chang Lan (all Vice-Chairmen), Huang Wen-pai, Kuo Mo-jo, Shen Yen-ping and other ministers. As all these are personalities of some consequence and so little is known outside about them a brief description may be of interest. Among the Vice-Chairmen, Chu Teh takes precedence over everyone else. He along with Mao Tse-tung was responsible for building up the People's Liberation Army, and for bringing it up to the present state of efficiency: for planning and organizing the great campaigns which destroyed the Kuomintang forces. Born of a farmer's family (one of thirteen) in Szechuan, Chu Teh was educated for military service and became an officer of the new army in 1909. In an article published in 1950 mourning the death of his mother, Chu Teh has described his early days and the difficulties his parents had to undergo to give him an education. From his childhood he seems to have been a revolutionary. It is an undoubted fact that he and his regiment vigorously opposed Yuan Shih kai's attempt to restore the monarchy. When the first revolution failed and the country became a prey to war lords, Chu Teh left for Europe for higher military studies. Then he became a communist and when the northern expedition was organized under the leadership of Chiang Kai-shek and with the co-operation of the communists, he was in command of a unit. It was only in 1928 that he stepped prominently on the stage of Chinese history, when in association with Chou En-lai he organized the revolt of Nanchang and thus laid the foundation of the People's Liberation Army. How he brought his ragged troops to join Mao Tse-tung and his band on the Ching Kan-shan mountains and how between them they organized the People's Liberation Army and resisted the successive annihilation campaigns of Chiang are well known. Today he is the hero of the Red Army, the genius behind its reorganization and the symbol of its hardihood and strength.

In appearance Chu Teh is short and stocky. There is nothing to differentiate him from the millions of Chinese peasants whom he has put in uniform. He is modest and retiring by nature. I remember once at a garden party in my house he quietly went by himself, after shaking hands with us, and sat in a pavilion with a few friends drinking beer and chatting pleasantly, without expecting any special courtesies or attention. When I went to call on him, the first thing I noticed was his extreme simplicity, and the naturalness of his conversation. Chu Teh is undoubtedly a great revolutionary leader, the joint creator of a mighty army, but I could not imagine him as a communist thinker. His present wife whom I met at an army day party is a young woman of not more than thirty-five. She had a romantic career, starting life as a domestic servant, from which condition of slavery she ran away to join the P.L.A. where as a sharp-shooter she became a legendary figure. In appearance she is a typical revolutionary woman, who makes no pretence to womanly graces.

Liu Shao-chi was at the time the recognized theoretician of the party after Mao Tse-tung. He is said to be the author of the scheme of land reform and of the general programme of socialization which guides the economic evolution of China. In any case he was more interested in the ideological aspect of the movement than in the practical working of government. We talked mainly of land reform and I found him reserved and dogmatic. The general idea at the time was that he was the designated successor to Mao Tse-tung. It was difficult for me to form any definite opinion about him, as I never was able to establish a contact of minds with him though during my stay in Peking I had occasion to meet him a number of times.

Of Li Chi-shen and Chang Lan there is very little one can profitably say. Li is the leader of the Kuomintang Revolutionaries. He was Chief of Staff to Chiang at one time and parted company with him after the war. Undoubtedly his defection helped the communist cause, but today, apart from his position as a Vice-Chairman, he does not seem to count for much. His wife is a lady of great charm, not in the least affected by communist fashions and still wearing elegant silks and costly jewellery. My wife became very good friends with her, as she was of the orthodox type and they found subjects of common interest to talk to each other. Chang Lan, the leader of the Democratic Party, is also more of an historic figure than a present force. The Democratic Party had a hold on the intellectuals at the time of the Kuomintang. They were determined opponents of Chiang, and did everything in their power to undermine him. In fact, the defection of intelligentsia from Chiang's leadership was to a large extent the work of the Democratic Party. Chang Lan is a "venerable ancient." He is over seventy-five,* an impressive figure, tall, well set-up with a fine beard and always dressed in flowing silk robes. He is a man of considerable intellectual power and was a professor before he took to politics.

Among the Vice-Premiers and Ministers whom I called on, three men are worthy of special mention: Kuo Mo-jo, Huang Wen-pai and Shen Ying-ping or Mo-Tan as he is known in literary circles. Kuo Mo-jo is what is called in China an unattached

* He passed away recently.

"democratic personage." He is certainly not a communist, though his democracy would appear to be of a kind which finds all the virtues in communism. A leading archaeologist and historian and a poet and writer who contributed a great deal to the literary renaissance of modern China, Kuo Mo-jo is a man of remarkable intellectual attainments. His main contribution in the field of archaeology was his interpretation of the Shang Bone writings, which carried back the authentic history of China by a thousand years. He is the President of the reconstituted *Acedmia Sinica* and may be said to be the leading intellectual in new China. Kuo Mo-jo is Mao Tse-tung's ambassador to all cultural gatherings, and the chief representative of China on the Peace Council. In his approach to cultural and intellectual matters I did not find that he had any communist prejudices. He admired the classics of the Tang period and at least in one conversation with me, he discussed with profound insight the relations of Chinese drama with early Indian theatre. He was undoubtedly high in favour with the Government, was the Vice-Premier in charge of cultural affairs and generally the spokesman of the regime when cultural delegations from other countries arrived in China.

Huang Wen-pai, the Vice-Premier in charge of light industries, is a different type of personality. He is the head of a minor party, which, during the civil war, had associated itself closely with the communists. When I visited Yenan a few months later, I was shown a note written by him which is preserved there, the meaning of which was as follows: "I may not live to see the Liberation of China, but when that day arrives, let it be remembered that I, Huang Wen-pai, visited Yenan three times." Huang is in many ways a cultured, patriotic mandarin of the old type, intensely proud of China and its ancient civilization, a believing Buddhist and a vegetarian! He is always ready with his quotation from the classics and his memory in this respect is extraordinary. One day I went to see him in connection with a passage which seemed obscure in an English translation of the famous drama *The Western Chamber*. I had only to indicate the passage to him and he quoted the whole and entered into a long discourse on the greatness of the work. I asked him politely what his attitude was to such "reactionary and feudalistic literature." He said: "It is a part of our Chinese inheritance. We are building up a new society, but it does not mean we discard or disown the achievements of our ancient civilization." Short, but broad-shouldered and with a twinkle in his eye, Vice-Premier Huang always seemed to me one of the most sympathetic personalities of new China.

Shen Ying-ping, better known by his pen name, Mo Tan, was the Minister of Culture. He is an outstanding novelist whose panoramic work in three volumes describes the rise, disintegration, and fall of the middle-class movement in China. He is something of an "exquisite," always dressed in elegant clothes, even when sporting the rather drab uniform of new China. A man of ability and understanding, he gave me the impression of being ill-adjusted mentally with his surroundings. Other interesting personalities who may be mentioned are Madame Shih Liang, the Minister of Justice, Madame Li Teh-chuan, the Minister of Public Health, and Shen Chun-ju, the Chief Justice. Shih Liang was one of the leading lawyers of China before she assumed her present post. Though a radical in her politics and a member of the Government, she does not evidently follow the communist directive about lipstick and make-up. Whenever I have had the pleasure of seeing her, she was dressed with great care and taste. She was one of the seven "men lawyers" whom Chiang Kai-shek arrested at one time for her outspoken opposition to the K.M.T. regime! Her husband who speaks English well has some kind of a post in the Foreign Office but is generally inconspicuous.

Madame Li is a different kind of personality. She is the widow of the "Christian General," Feng Yu-hsiang, whose life ended tragically on a ship in the Black Sea while returning from the United States. Madame Li is a picture of quiet efficiency, makes no pretence of being elegant or well dressed but is obviously full of energy and competence.

Shen Chun-ju, the famous jurist, is a strange-looking man. Hardly five feet in height, with an elongated head, flowing beards on both sides of his chin, he gives one the impression of deformity. But a few minutes of conversation are enough to show that this strange head contains an amazingly powerful brain and his bright eyes are capable of acute observation.

These were among the first people I met in New China and generally speaking I gained the impression that the Central People's Government was being run by men and women who were efficient and honest, who knew their minds and were prepared to put their best into the service of the State. There was a dynamism in all of them, a desire to go forward, which is perhaps the characteristic of all new Governments. It was significant, however, that it was not a government of youth. They had been tried and tested over a period of years and none of the leading personalities seemed under fifty.

CHAPTER VII

OFFICIAL RECEPTIONS

A WEEK after I had presented my credentials, I received an invitation from Mao Tse-tung to a banquet in my honour. The first thing that surprised me was that my wife was not included in the invitation. In new China it appeared that wives do not generally take part in official functions unless they hold official positions themselves. The dinner was timed for six o'clock. In these and in other matters New China has discarded Western fashions. Though it was an official banquet no dress had been prescribed. It was to the palace on the lake where I had presented my credentials that the officers of the protocol took me. The lake itself had been emptied and was dry. The soil was being removed in lorries by units of the People's Liberation Army, to serve as manure in the fields outside the city. My companion explained to me that they were beautifying the lake by opening canals and keeping the water fresh. The "Ocean Terrace," the tiny artificial island on the lake where the reforming Emperor Kang Hsu was imprisoned and allowed to die a slow death, lay to our right. The yellow tiles of its roof shone like a mass of molten gold in the rays of the setting sun but the reflection in the water which gave it an unearthly beauty when I saw it last, was absent as the lake was dry.

On arrival I was received by the Director of Ceremonies and escorted to the drawing-room where I found waiting for me all the Vice-Chairmen including General Chu Teh, the Prime Minister and the senior Vice Foreign Minister, Chang Han-fu. Mao Tse-tung himself, though the nominal host, was absent. I was told that he had not been keeping well and therefore was avoiding all dinners and other evening functions. It was Chu Teh who played the host.

We spent a little time talking of general things. I was plied with innumerable questions about industrial conditions and social changes in India. It was Chou En-lai and Liu Shao-chi who asked most of the questions with Chu Teh putting in a word now and then. The dinner itself was a very interesting function. It was of course Chinese food that was served, but the *hors d'œuvre* was spread in the Soviet fashion. The table was loaded with delicacies and we began as usual with toasts in Chinese rice wine to the friendship between India and China, the success of my mission, etc. For all the cordiality and pleasant conversation there was an air of artificial restraint and I could sense a feeling of uncertainty in the minds of my hosts as to how far they should go in their attitude of cordiality towards me.

A few days later there was a formal reception to all the diplomats at the Foreign Office. It was one of the most curious functions that I have ever attended. We were all received at the head of the stairs by Chou En-lai and Madame Chou. The first curious thing I noticed was that everyone, except the Danish Minister who was in tails, was dressed most informally. The Chinese guests, who were mostly officials of the Foreign Office and those selected for service abroad, were in loose fitting close coats and trousers which constitute the official uniform for both men and women. Some of the higher officials looked distinguished even in this dress but the general impression was one of calculated untidiness. The impression I gained—at the first party—was that the communists went through it as a matter of unpleasant duty. There was no conversation, no atmosphere of friendliness. After the dinner was over we were led into a hall where we were entertained with two propaganda films.

After this official reception, a friendly dinner party specially for us came as a pleasant surprise. Barely a week after the reception we were invited by Chou En-lai and his wife and I steeled myself for the same impersonal entertainment as we had to suffer before. But everything was different this time. The wives of the Chinese officials were there, all suitably dressed in long silk gowns— newly made, as one could see. Madame Chou, whom we came to know and admire later, was all graciousness and the conversation before dinner was friendly, cheerful and pleasant.

There was warmth and cordiality in the atmosphere which we greatly appreciated.

The dinner was in the Chinese style with innumerable courses, but I was happy to see them served in dishes and not kept in the centre with each one taking what he wanted with the chopsticks with which he had already eaten. A mature and delicious Che-kiang wine was served in small glasses and toasts followed with appropriate speeches. After the meal was over we sat out on the terrace and talked about things in general. Chou En-lai spoke to me of his days in Chungking where he was stationed as Mao Tse-tung's envoy to the National Government during the years of war. He alluded to Pandit Nehru's visit to Chungking and how he was sorry to have missed him. The conversation turned on Chiang Kai-shek and I told him that in my view Chiang was a patriot, but that his mind was medieval and that he viewed things from a narrow point of view. Chou would not give him credit for enlightened patriotism even of the bourgeois type. Chiang's attitude, declared Chou, was monarchical, that is, he was attached to China only so long as he and China were synonymous.

I asked him about the famous Sian incident when Chiang Kai-shek was arrested by the young marshal. It was as a result of Chou En-lai's intervention that Chiang was then released from captivity. So much everyone knows. I wanted to try and get Chou's version of the incident. He talked quite freely about it and said that in the then circumstances (1936) his party was convinced that the leadership of Chiang Kai-shek was necessary in national interests. "There was no one else who was in a position to organize national resistance against Japan. The other leaders of the Kuomin-tang, especially Ho Ying-chin and his friends, were for a com-promise with Japan. We had no doubt that united national opposition to Japan was the first step towards the liberation of China and this could then have been organized only under Chiang's leadership. To have shot him, as the young marshal threatened, would have been disastrous." Such was the gist of his argument.

Another subject of interest which I raised with him was about the historic insurrection in Shanghai in 1927 when he was the

Deputy Commander of the rebels. I asked why the revolutionaries had allowed themselves to be crushed after they had practically taken over Shanghai. Chou replied: "We had not anticipated the revolutionary enthusiasm of the people. Our leadership was in-experienced. We did not know either how to exploit our success or the tactics of retreat. The Shanghai workers and the peasants of the neighbouring countryside were ready: but we did not have the machinery of co-operation ready. So Chiang was able to crush us."

This dinner was a great success and established the first social contact between us.

253791

CHAPTER VIII

LIFE IN PEKING. I

D IPLOMATIC life in Peking was organized in an unusual way. Apart from the now normal division between the Soviet *bloc* diplomats and the representatives of the western powers Peking had three further groups: those non-communist countries who had recognized China and maintained diplomatic missions, those who had recognized but were still negotiating diplomatic representation, and those who had not recognized but had kept some official in charge of their affairs. The first group consisted of India, Burma, Pakistan, Indonesia, Denmark, Sweden, Switzerland and Finland. Those who had recognized but had only negotiating envoys included the United Kingdom, Holland and Norway. The Belgian, French and Italian representatives were not recognized and had no diplomatic status. There was a further complication. There were a number of missions in Peking which the non-communist world did not recognize. North Korea and Outer Mongolia had regular ambassadors with unusually large staffs. Viet Minh and East Germany maintained permanent "delegations" whose heads had the rank of ambassadors. The confusion resulting from this multiplicity of status and recognition and non-recognition of missions may well be imagined. The negotiating representatives, e.g. of Britain, were not recognized as belonging to the diplomatic corps as their relations were not with the Government but only with the Foreign Office, for the purpose of a specific negotiation. The Chinese officials, excepting the Foreign Minister and those connected with the negotiations, pretended not to know them and it was therefore embarrassing to have them at the same party. The representatives of the States which had not recognized China were of course outside the pale. The Korean, the Mongolian, and the Viet Minh Ambassadors were at all Chinese parties, but we did not recognize them in public and they also took no notice of us. Slowly, however, I was able to establish relations on a personal basis with the Mongolians and with the Viet Minh representatives. The position of a country like India was especially difficult as it had to be on friendly relations with everyone. I had therefore to arrange my life in compartments so that no one could feel embarrassed or for that matter have any grounds for complaint.

The Asian representatives made a small nucleus of their own and we were therefore able to hold the balance in the social sphere. The Burmese Ambassador, Mynt Thein, was a diplomat of remarkable personal charm whose wife, an able and educated lady, was popular in all circles. Monty, as he was known, had an exceptional gift for looking at the bright side of things, but as a diplomat he was shrewd, observant, and far-seeing. Indonesia was represented by a chargé d'affaires, Izzak Mahdi, who had been a guerrilla fighter in the war of independence and was radical in his political views. He spoke practically every European language. We worked closely together and I found Mahdi well informed and wise. The representatives of European States which maintained full diplomatic missions were of course career diplomatists. Among them, the most effective was Clement Rezzonnico, the Swiss Minister, who carried out with conscientious thoroughness his country's policy of neutrality. Rezzonnico's main concern was humanitarian: to see that the missionaries and foreign nationals who had no diplomatic protection received fair treatment or at least were afforded facilities to go out of the country.

The Soviet *bloc* representatives were of course the most prominent in Peking. Of these, N. V. Roschin, the Soviet Ambassador, had been my colleague in Nanking. He was a general in the army and had been previously military attaché at Chungking. His knowledge of Chinese politics was, therefore, intimate. He was in many ways a very helpful man, discussed public affairs freely within the limits of his position, and, as doyen of the corps, was willing at all times to help other diplomats with advice. During my two years of stay in Peking I found him a sympathetic and helpful colleague. The Polish Ambassador, Burgin, was also a pleasant and friendly diplomat. He had been an underground fighter during the war and he often regaled me with stories of his experiences in Warsaw during the German occupation. The most interesting of the "New Democratic" Ambassadors was Wezikopf, who was the head of the Czechoslovak Mission. He was a novelist and writer who had spent many years in the United States. I do not know whether he was a communist; his wife in any case did not seem to be. She was a writer of children's stories, a chic and charming lady from Vienna, whose attitude towards life one could easily notice from her behaviour. Wezikopf had much of the European spirit which is a characteristic of Czech intellectuals and looked at things sometimes from that point of view. In any case, unlike the other Soviet group Ambassadors, he did not pretend that everything was wrong in non-communist countries and it was a pleasure to discuss general historical and political questions with him.

When I reached Peking the British negotiating representative was John (later Sir John) Hutchison. Hutchison had been Commercial Minister in Nanking under Sir Ralph Stevenson. He was an excellent man, but did not claim to be much of a politician. He was replaced later by Sir Leo Lamb, a totally different type of diplomatist. Leo Lamb was an old China hand in the best sense of the term who had started in China as a Vice-Consul in some distant town and had seen continuous service in the country. He had witnessed the marriage of Emperor Pu Yi in the Forbidden City, had seen the Manchu nobles and court functionaries *Kotow* to the Son of Heaven (then exercising his authority within the palace), had known most of the war lords in their time and had watched the rise and fall of the Kuomintang fortunes and had even been imprisoned by the Japanese. He spoke Chinese well and was greatly interested in Chinese culture. But his sympathies were all with the old mandarins, the cultured leisurely class of the past who had given so much distinction to social life in China. A conservative to the core, he had but little sympathy with the changes in China and seemed almost to regret the disappearance of the Empire. He was in no sense against Chinese nationalism, but it seemed to me that he found it difficult to adjust his mind to the changed conditions in China. With him and his wife our relations were excellent and I benefited greatly from his unrivalled know-ledge and experience.

At all times Peking had more than its share of eccentrics. Previously, in the days of extra-territoriality, their number and variety constituted one of the attractions of Peking. With the Japanese occupation many of them had gone back to their own countries. With the communists in power, the atmosphere was even less congenial and yet some of them continued to live their lives unperturbed by political changes. The most interesting of all the eccentrics I met in Peking (or elsewhere) was Vincenz Hund-hausen, poet, musician, pamphleteer and master printer, who had forsaken the world and lived on an artificial island outside the city wall. Hundhausen, who is a baron of Prussia, was a lawyer in Berlin before the first war and came out to China to settle some legal affairs for a big German firm. What he did for his clients I do not know but Peking cast its spell on him and he announced his intention not to return to Europe. He bought some marshy land, and an island home for himself, planted poplar trees around it so that it was totally invisible from outside, and established himself there like a feudal baron, surrounded by his tenants and depen-dants. From the grounds, the outside world could not be seen at all; but from the terrace of the little house one could see the Western Hills glistening in snow in winter or changing colours like chame-leons in spring time.

There on that island he established the best printing press in China, with matrices specially made in Germany, and devoted himself to the popularization of Chinese literature. His translations of *The Western Chamber* and other Chinese classics into German verse are said to be of high quality. In any case they were printed by him on beautiful rice paper and bound in Chinese style. Hundhausen was a regular maniac when it came to missionary activity. You had only to mention the subject for him to rise up in anger and declaim about the misfortunes that missionaries had brought on the world.

The Kuomintang during their last days ruined his dream island. During the siege of Peking in 1948, the K.M.T. General cut down the magnificent trees surrounding the island, and the old man, then seventy-three, had to be carried away by force into the city, so that, left alone in the deserted island with armies on both sides, he might not starve and die. After the communists occupied Peking, he was allowed to return, but the Kuomintang had looted his press and there was nothing left of it. Also a new kind of trouble had overtaken him. After the communist occupation, his tenants became the proprietors of their plots. The old man had therefore only the dilapidated house left to him.

There he lived alone, but his spirit was unbroken and he had a mind that was still extremely vigorous. In appearance he was indeed striking. Over six feet tall, still erect and military and Prussian in his bearing in spite of his seventy-five years, with a leonine head and a defiant look, Hundhausen challenged the world and its vanities. He had only a part-time cook-attendant. In fact he had cut his needs to a minimum and was entirely at peace with himself. When I went to see him one afternoon he told me that he had not seen a visitor for eight weeks. The house, which was in a state of utter disrepair, where one was constantly afraid that the staircase may collapse or the roof fall, was literally covered with books on which the dust of ages had collected. There were books in German, Russian, French, English and Chinese—thousands of them with a complete first-edition Voltaire and all the German classics, some of them in the finest binding. The poetry, drama, philosophy of European nations and the Chinese were adequately represented. In fact it was difficult to move about in the house, because of books.

I always found a conversation with him invigorating, because in spite of the dirt and insanitary conditions of his surroundings Hundhausen struck me as being something of a Yogi—a Yogi who is still at war with prejudice and superstition but with a mind that is calm and detached. The wines in the house were brewed by himself. He wore the padded long gown of the Chinese, and ate their food, and lived unconcerned with what was happening in the world.

No less interesting a personage was my friend William Empson, the poet and critic, who was then professor of English at the Peking National University. Empson, with his wife Hetta, a noted sculptor, lived in a Chinese house near the University. The British community—forgetting that he was undoubtedly the most distinguished Englishman in Peking at the time—disapproved of his way of life and his refusal to conform to the suburban habits of its diplomats. Empson sported a strange type of beard, kept company with doubtful Chinese, and allowed his children to play in the backyards of Chinese houses where they grew up uninhibited. His house, in a not very clean part of Peking, was always more untidy than even the habitation of Hundhausen. There Ezra Pound's Pisan Cantos, textbooks, detective novels and proofs of Empson's own *Structure of the Complex World* lay cheek by jowl with toys of children, Chinese new year paintings, and half finished sculptures by Hetta. Empson had been an intimate friend of Orwell and we had many interests in common. It was a matter of some speculation among my colleagues as to what I should find in common with the Empsons. Then someone gave it out that I was also a poet of some standing in my own language and that is said to have satisfied the stuffed shirts among my colleagues.

There was one other personality then in Peking who deserves some mention. This was the famous Madame Dan, a Manchu noblewoman of the *ancien régime*. She and her sister the famous Princess Derling were noted beauties at the Imperial Court before the revolution. The Emperor Kang Hsu is even said to have offered "marriage" to Madame Dan. Anyway she was lady in waiting to the Dowager Empress Tzu Hsi, the Old Buddha, and survived the Imperial regime to become the director of ceremonies to Yuan Shih-kai, a post which she claims to have held till the capital was shifted by the Kuomintang to Nanking. When that happened she opened an exclusive curio shop, for she had indeed exquisite taste and was able to obtain genuine treasures from old Manchu princely and noble families. As she spoke perfect English, French, and Japanese and had further the prestige of having been an important member of the old Manchu nobility she was a popular figure in the large cosmopolitan colony in Peking at the time and is said to have made a fortune by selling curios to visiting foreigners. But those happy days soon came to a close when the Japanese took over Peking. It is not quite clear how she carried on during that time, but according to her the Japanese took away all the good things she had and she was reduced to comparative poverty.

When the communists took over there was nothing to do for a Manchu princess. Besides she was over seventy years old and miserably poor. However they did not interfere with her and she eked out a living by giving French lessons to the women of the diplomatic colony. But even in her poverty she went about with her head high. To all the diplomatic parties she was invited she arrived looking the picture of old-world grace, her head beautifully coiffured and wearing the magnificent silk gowns of earlier days. Perhaps the jades she wore were not genuine, but who cared? She was amazingly beautiful at the age of seventy, straight backed, without a wrinkle on her face, dressed as if she were in attendance on the Empress. Her husband "General" Dan, an insignificant looking Cantonese, followed her dutifully everywhere.

Madame Dan was not only a beautiful woman with all the graces and charms of high aristocracy, but a very courageous one. That she was poor as a church mouse everyone knew, but when she was invited to a house she came as a princess. She was gay and amusing, prepared at her age to give an exhibition of sword dancing and other accomplishments. But she had one innocent weakness. She had invented a lot of stories about herself, including one which claimed that her mother was American! Photographs of her Manchu mother with the Empress have been published in many books. In fact everyone knew that she was a pure-blooded Manchu and yet she was anxious to impress the foreigners by claiming an American mother. Of the stories of the Imperial Court which she invented and circulated there was no end. These I suspect were the results of old age.

Madame Dan was a great favourite with my family. To us she was a survival of a vanished age and we were able to understand many things about old China by conversations with her. My daughter pretended to take lessons from her in French. That gave her not only a little money but an occupation which she could report to the authorities, for in China everyone is supposed to work, and unless you have an occupation you may be allotted work which you do not like or written down as a reactionary.

The thing that impressed me most in Peking was the extraordinary building activity that was going on. The communists were anxious not to interfere with the beauty of old Peking. So far as the old buildings like the Forbidden City, the Temple of Heaven, and the Temple of Confucius were concerned, the communists concerned themselves mainly with repairs and with undoing the neglect of the past. In a short time they had cleared away the accumulated dirt of the Pei Hai, the beautiful series of artificial lakes in the centre of the city. Fine parks were laid out on its shores and even the white Pagoda on the top of the hill was repaired and repainted. Their main building activity, however, was in the area where the Japanese had originally intended to erect a new city. A *cité universitaire* was erected there to accommodate the educational and research institutions of Peking. An industrial town was also erected near Pa Man Chan. In fact New Peking, outside the city wall and extending to the Summer Palace, was to be a model city with People's Universities and new style workers' residences —a symbol of the constructive activities of the communist era.

The Summer Palace was transformed into a workers' paradise. Rebuilt by the Dowager Empress to replace the magnificent palace and pleasure gardens of Chien Lung, which the European nations in a moment of atavistic relapse had burnt down, the Summer Palace was a series of gardens and pavilions set in an unimaginably beautiful background of hills and streams. The palace faced a lake which is said to have been constructed artificially. There are innumerable small pavilions, pagodas, shaded walks, and lotus pools in this former imperial retreat. After the capital was shifted to Nanking, the Summer Palace, like the Forbidden City itself, was left uncared for. Its pavilions were let out for nominal rents to foreigners as bungalows for summer or for week-end amusements. The new regime wasted no time in turning the place into a workers' resort. One side of the lake was converted into a beautiful *plage* which on Saturdays and Sundays is crowded by students and trade unionists who are brought from

Peking in special lorries. Organized expeditions bring thousands of P.L.A. men and workers who picnic in the gardens and sing and play in groups. What the Old Buddha would have thought of this we can but imagine.

Another act of the new regime which pleased me greatly was the attention it paid to that structure of unique beauty, the Temple of Heaven. When I visited it in 1948 under the Kuomintang the sight it presented was something which would have broken the heart of the coldest philistine. Refugee "students" from the north-east had taken possession of the place and had converted the whole place into a filthy and evil smelling lavatory. Later I heard that General Fu Tso-yi had, in order to construct an air-strip, cut down a great many of the old and noble trees with which the temple was surrounded. The communists cleaned up the place, planted new trees where they had been cut down, and restored the temple to its original beauty.

But they were not so sensitive about other buildings. The so-called Temple of Agriculture was converted into a stadium, and in the Temple of Confucius they established, perhaps appropriately, a police school. The great Lama Temple was left untouched, perhaps in consideration of the religious sentiments of the Mongolian and Tibetan Buddhists. But, the Central Park, attached to the Forbidden City, was converted into a great centre of attraction, and the avenue of wistaria and the peony gardens blossomed again for the benefit of the Peking public. The Temple of Ancestors in the Forbidden City became the workers' palace with an immense open-air theatre, and with facilities for recreation, amusement, and study. Generally it was clear that the new regime was anxious to cater for the working classes.

When I took up my political work the first thing I noticed was that apart from Chou En-lai and some of his close associates, especially Chen Chia-kang, no one in China knew anything about India. They had only vague ideas about India's political position or historical development. Most people in China had a romantic interest in India—the inheritance of the Buddhist tradition—but no one knew anything of modern India. This was not only due to the notorious egocentrism of the Chinese, but because their educa-

tion in the past had been controlled by the Americans and to a
lesser extent by western missionary societies. Their knowledge, as
of ours in India, was more of western countries than of their
eastern neighbours. Besides, the leaders of the new regime had been
living mostly in inaccessible areas engaged in guerrilla warfare,
and such information as they possessed came exclusively from
communist sources. But soon I discovered that the Chinese were
anxious to know about India. They were in two minds. Instinc-
tively they recognized that India was friendly to them; but as
communists they could only think of India as a capitalist country,
and by all textbook maxims it seemed clear that India must be
reactionary and must belong to the opposite camp. The first
indication I had of their desire to know more about India was
when I received an invitation to speak on India to the Foreign
Office officials. This was an exceptional favour, and I took advantage of the opportunity to emphasize the anti-imperialist character
of India's struggle, the common sufferings of the people of Asia
and therefore the common conditioning of their mind towards
the world, the common problems of raising standards of life, etc.
The talk, I was later informed by Chang Han-fu, the Vice-
Minister, had an excellent effect. Soon, I was asked to deliver a
formal address to the Institute of International Relations and the
subject I chose was the motivations of the Indian Revolution.

CHAPTER IX

KOREA

WHEN I came to Peking I had imagined my mission to be nothing more than that of witnessing the development of a revolution and of working for a better understanding between China and India. I knew, like everyone else, that with a communist China cordial and intimate relations were out of the question, but I was fairly optimistic about working out an area of co-operation by eliminating causes of misunderstanding, rivalry, etc. The only area where our interests overlapped was in Tibet, and knowing the importance that every Chinese Government, including the Kuomintang, had attached to exclusive Chinese authority over that area I had, even before I started for Peking, come to the conclusion that the British policy (which we were supposed to have inherited) of looking upon Tibet as an area in which we had special political interests could not be maintained. The Prime Minister had also in general agreed with this view. So there was nothing which I could then foresee that would make my mission unduly difficult, exciting, or troublesome. I had every reason to feel that an excellent opportunity was given to me to watch the revolution from a vantage ground and to see an historical drama of the highest importance being acted in front of me by men and women whom I knew personally.

These pleasant expectations suffered a rude shock when one day in the last week of June, 1950, the Chinese newspapers announced that the South Koreans had crossed the frontier, that war had as a result broken out between the two Koreas. The next day the wireless announced the historic decision of President Truman to send American troops to the support of the South Koreans, who equally claimed to be the victims of aggression, and further to take Taiwan under the protection of the seventh American fleet. After that events moved fast. The Security Council (in the absence of the Soviets, and with Egypt abstaining and India hesitating) declared that the North Koreans were the aggressors and authorized the United States to enforce the necessary sanctions. Thus the war in Korea started on an international basis.

From the beginning I attached much greater importance to Truman's action in respect of Taiwan than to the United Nations intervention in Korea, because essentially it seemed to me that the United States had willy-nilly as a result of the Korean incident stepped directly into the Chinese civil war, which had effectively ended with the flight of the Kuomintang forces from the mainland. U.N. intervention in Korea caused no particular reaction in China: in fact during the first three months of the Korean war there was hardly any noticeable military activity in China. But the intervention in Taiwan was considered to be a direct threat, though even in this matter the Chinese behaved with exemplary patience and restraint. For many days after the Korean war started, there was nothing in the atmosphere of Peking to give anyone the impression that anything unusual had happened. While the United States and generally the western nations were behaving as if the heavens were falling there was absolute calm in Peking— a very strange and unnatural situation.

July the 1st was the twenty-ninth anniversary of the communist party of China. It was being celebrated with the usual display of flags and all the paraphernalia of party enthusiasm. It was on that day that India made the first move in Peking which was to take us along the hard road of peace-makers, sending us finally to Korea to guard the prisoners of war and to sponsor the explanations. I called at the Foreign Office and had a long talk with Chang Han-fu, the Vice Foreign Minister. I impressed on him the necessity of localizing the Korean conflict and put forward tentatively the suggestion that the question could probably be solved by referring it to the Security Council, with China taking her legitimate place, and consequently the Soviets giving up their boycott and returning to their vacant seat. I did not mention to him that Prime Minister Nehru had already moved Bevin in this connection. Chang Han-fu seemed to receive the suggestion very sympathetically and promised to let me know his Government's reaction soon.

In the meantime a touch of comedy was added to the situation. Chiang Kai-shek came forward with an offer of 25,000 troops to fight in Korea, as in spite of MacArthur's heroic gestures with his air force and the brutal bombardments of Korean coastal towns by the ships of the two greatest naval powers, the northern forces were advancing steadily. But Chiang's offer was politely declined on the ground that the troops might be required for the defence of Formosa itself.

On the 10th of July the Chinese Government officially replied to my representation expressing appreciation of the line that India had taken and conveying general agreement with our proposals. My first reaction was that perhaps a way had been found for settling the problem before it became too serious; but on second thoughts I realized that the proposal of seating Peking in the Security Council, however legitimate, reasonable, and logical, would be resisted by the Americans since it would involve an immense loss of face to them. It was also obvious that in the face of definite American opposition Bevin would not be able to act. Still there was a chance, and on receiving the Chinese reactions, Mr. Nehru formally put forward these proposals to Stalin and Acheson.

Stalin replied immediately, accepting the proposal on "the indispensable condition" of the Peking Government being given its seat on the Security Council. That the Russians did not expect anything to come out of this was clear from the fact that *Tass* published the correspondence before Acheson had a chance to reply. Acheson of course turned down the proposal on the ground that the question of Peking's membership of the Security Council was unrelated to the Korean issue!

It is of course impossible to write in any detail about the diplomatic activities connected with the Korean war as they are still in the realm of state secrets, and considerable time must elapse before the telegrams and despatches connected with this important chapter of history could be published.

By the middle of July the Chinese attitude towards the Korean war began to show a change. There was evidence of a planned campaign to bring home to the public what the communists considered to be the character of American intervention in Asia. Cartoons, paintings on the wall, articles in newspapers were all now directed against "the aggressive American forces in Korea." The American campaign to secure international support for their action in Asia was also the subject of much sarcastic comment. The anti-climax of this American campaign came, much to the amusement of the Chinese, with the announcements of Romulo and Pibul Songgram offering the services of their armed forces. Brigadier Romulo was sorry that he could not spare any regular forces, but was willing to permit recruitment of volunteers, no doubt at American rates of pay. Pibul Songgram, as he is a marshal, went one step further and offered 5,000 Siamese troops. With Siam and the Philippines actively co-operating, America was able to claim that the free nations of Asia were behind her, even if India, Pakistan, Burma, and Indonesia gave no support.

One thing which impressed me greatly during these months was the moderation and restraint of the Chinese. While it was true that their propaganda against the Americans was bitter in tone, there was no attempt to work up a feeling of chauvinism. There were, however, constant allusions to the immediate necessity of "liberating" Taiwan and Tibet. The last was naturally causing me concern. On the 22nd of August Chou En-lai sent for me, for a general discussion, and I took the opportunity of pressing home the desirability of restraint and moderation in regard to Taiwan, especially when the whole world was inclined to view their case with favour. In regard to Tibet, I knew they were a little uncertain about our attitude. I expressed the hope that they would follow a policy of peace in regard to Tibet. Chou En-lai replied that while the liberation of Tibet was a "sacred duty," his Government were anxious to secure their ends by negotiations and not by military action. He said that he had heard that the Nepal Government had offered to send troops to help the Tibetans and wondered if it was true! That was the state of Chinese knowledge about the conditions on the Himalayan border.

My main activity at this time was concentrated on emphasizing to the Indian Government that it should get the situation in respect of Taiwan clarified, for I was afraid that the Chinese might be led into some rash action to "liberate" that island. This would bring them into direct conflict with America. Some conversations with the Polish Ambassador had given me an indication that the Chinese were actively engaged in preparing for an invasion. I had also heard that the famous general Chen Yi had taken up his headquarters in Amoy where he was building up an air force and concentrating his strength on the Fukien coast. What I felt was that if the Chinese were rash enough to attempt an invasion a major conflict with America could not be avoided. The essential thing therefore appeared to be to allay Chinese fears about the nature of American actions in respect of Taiwan. The pressure that Prime Minister Nehru was able to exercise directly and through Whitehall had the desired effect. During the last week of August, the American Government issued no less than five statements on Taiwan, the last of which practically said that once the Korean issue was settled, America would withdraw her protecting hands from Taiwan. Acheson followed this up with a statement that America had no aggressive intentions against the mainland of China. The situation seemed to ease a little.

On the 2nd of September Chou En-lai came to dine with me privately. He brought his wife with him, an exceptional act of courtesy, as Madame Chou does not keep good health and generally does not go out for parties. I had also asked my friend Mynt Thein, the Burmese Ambassador, with whom I had worked closely in Nanking. The dinner went off extremely well, Mynt Thein keeping the whole party roaring with laughter with his stories. Chou En-lai, unaccustomed I presume to this kind of diplomatic dinner, relaxed completely and kept on saying in English that it was a "homely party." The conversation at the table was witty and amusing, if not brilliant, mainly through the irrepressible good humour of the Burmese Ambassador and the cordial expansiveness of Chou En-lai himself.

After the dinner Chou En-lai, the Burmese Ambassador and myself sat apart and the conversation became serious. As the host I did not want to take the initiative in discussing political matters.

So the ice was broken by the Burmese Ambassador. The conversation was mainly about China's relations with the outside world and we both emphasized that their present policies had only tended to isolate China from neutral opinion. I said: "It may be that you think that there is no neutral opinion: in my view there is not only a neutral opinion but considerable pro-Chinese feeling in countries like India and Burma, and even in England where many influential groups are anxious to understand the Chinese point of view. Actually, China has enforced a blockade against herself so far as the non-communist world is concerned." The Burmese Ambassador suggested that they should send good-will missions to the South Asian countries and find out for themselves—a suggestion which impressed Chou En-lai and was in principle accepted by him with enthusiasm.

Mynt Thein saw that he had scored a point and we thought that the time was appropriate to press for a modification of the violent propaganda against America which was then going on in China. Mynt Thein's line was that China had already scored a notable victory by getting the Security Council to hear her case against American aggression in Taiwan and over the air space of Manchuria and now it was in China's interest to cultivate world opinion by the moderation of her point of view. By nature Chou En-lai is a reasonable man. He is also a most persuasive talker. Our talks went on till half-past eleven and on the whole both parties had reason to be satisfied.

The situation in Korea changed all of a sudden by the American landings at Inchon. There were great rejoicings in the western camp in China, and if the Chinese on their part were bitterly disappointed they showed no signs of it. When the northern lines began to be rolled up and the Americans and their allies were shouting of victory, my thoughts were all on Taiwan, for I felt that if the Americans were able to carry everything before them in Korea they might be tempted to encourage Chiang to attack the mainland and thus precipitate a world war. The situation seemed altogether confused. There were rumours of large-scale troop movements from the Peking area to the north, and a western Military Attaché told me that he had information that a continuous stream of troop trains was passing Tientsin. It was when things were in this state of uncertainty that General Nieh Yen-jung, the acting Chief of Staff who was also the Military Governor of Peking, with the inoffensive title of mayor, came to dine with me on the 25th of September. General Nieh, with his round face and shaven head, gives one the impression of a Prussian officer. But he is a pleasant-spoken man, friendly and ready to discuss matters with an air of frankness. After the dinner the conversation turned to Korea. General Nieh told me in a quiet and unexcited manner that the Chinese did not intend to sit back with folded hands and let the Americans come up to their border. This was the first indication I had that the Chinese proposed to intervene in the war. I was taken aback a little by this statement, all the more impressive because it was said in a quiet and pleasant tone, as if he were telling me that he intended to go shooting the next day. I asked him whether he realized in full the implications of such an action. He replied: "We know what we are in for, but at all costs American aggression has to be stopped. The Americans can bomb us, they can destroy our industries, but they cannot defeat us on land."

I tried to impress on him how destructive a war with America would be; how the Americans would be able to destroy systematically all the industries of Manchuria and put China back by half a century, how China's coastal towns would be exposed to bombardment and how even the interior could be bombed. He only laughed. "We have calculated all that," he said. "They may even drop atom bombs on us. What then? They may kill a few million people. Without sacrifice a nation's independence cannot be upheld." He gave some calculations of the effectiveness of atom bombs and said: "After all, China lives on the farms. What can atom bombs do there? Yes, our economic development will be put back. We may have to wait for it."

This conversation left me very depressed. The next morning I had some news which added greatly to that depression. After the general had left my house, my first secretary A. K. Sen had stayed for a time with me to enable us to compare notes. He left at about a quarter-past eleven but found that a curfew had been clamped on Peking and all traffic had been stopped. He was, however, escorted by a security officer to the Legation street but could not get back to his hotel. He was nevertheless able to see troop formations and trucks moving towards the railway station. Perhaps this was part of the general troop movements towards the Manchurian border.

The 1st of October celebrations passed off quietly. They started off with a reception by Mao Tse-tung where for the first and last time I saw Madame Mao. She stood at the head of the receiving line, a pretty, youngish woman of about forty, dressed elegantly but in no way different from the rest. With her stood Chou En-lai and his wife, while the Chairman and the Vice-Chairmen, including Madame Sun Yat-sen, were inside the hall and received us there. The reception was a quiet one and there were no speeches. The parade in the Red Square in front of the Gate of Heavenly Peace the next day was of course a grand affair, a display of the military might of New China. The function was interminably long, though it was picturesque and highly impressive. We had all expected to hear a definite declaration of policy but on that matter we were disappointed. Not for long however.

At midnight on the 2nd of October, after I had been asleep for an hour and a half, I was awakened by my steward with the news that Chen Chia-kang the Director of the Asian Affairs of the Foreign Ministry, was waiting for me in the drawing-room. I hastily put on my dressing-gown and went downstairs, not knowing what it could be which had brought so important an officer at midnight to my house. Chen was very apologetic about the lateness of the hour but added that the matter was most important and that the Prime Minister desired to see me immediately at his residence. I said I would be ready to accompany him in ten minutes and went upstairs to dress. When my wife heard that I was going out in the company of a Foreign Office official at that unusual time she was uncertain whether she was awake and witnessing my arrest and deportation or seeing a nightmare. It took me some time to persuade her that it was not usual to kidnap ambassadors and in my case she need not lose even a wink of sleep for fear that the Chinese would do any personal harm to me.

We left my house at twenty minutes past midnight. The streets were practically deserted and the clear October air in Peking added serenity to the silence of the night. Though I had guessed from the beginning that the reason for this sudden call was something connected with Korea, I was bursting with impatience to know what the matter actually was. Was it that Chou En-lai had fresh proposals that he desired to be communicated to Nehru? Was it to let me know that war had already started? Anyway I decided to wait and not to try and get an inkling from Chen. So we conversed about the magnificence of the celebrations of the previous day and the order and discipline which marked the proceedings. At 12.30 I was with Premier Chou En-lai at his official residence.

Though the occasion was the most serious I could imagine, a midnight interview on questions affecting the peace of the world, Chou En-lai was as courteous and charming as ever and did not give the least impression of worry or nervousness or indeed of being in any particular hurry. He had the usual tea served and the first two minutes were spent in normal courtesies, apology for disturbing me at an unusual hour, etc. Then he came to the point. He thanked Pandit Nehru for what he had been doing in the cause of peace, and said no country's need for peace was greater than that of China, but there were occasions when peace could only be defended by determination to resist aggression. If the Americans crossed the 38th parallel China would be forced to intervene in Korea. Otherwise he was most anxious for a peaceful settlement, and generally accepted Pandit Nehru's approach to the question. I asked him whether he had already news of the Americans having crossed the borders. He replied in the affirmative but added that he did not know where they had crossed. I asked him whether China intended to intervene, if only the South Koreans crossed the parallel. He was emphatic: "The South Koreans did not matter but American intrusion into North Korea would encounter Chinese resistance."

I returned home at 1.30 where my first secretary and cypher assistant were waiting. A telegram conveying the gist of the conversation with my own appreciation of the situation went the same night to New Delhi. I was fully satisfied that as Chou En-lai had claimed that the Americans had crossed the parallel, the Chinese troops which had been concentrated in Manchuria had also moved across the Yalu into North Korean territory. In the morning I contacted Hutchison, the British Minister, and told him briefly how matters stood. The Burmese Ambassador, who called later, was also kept informed and he also agreed to inform Thakin Nu immediately.

Nothing very much happened during the following two days. There was no definite information that the Americans had crossed the parallel. But the U.N. with historical insouciance was discussing a resolution to authorize MacArthur to cross the parallel and bring about the unification of Korea. On the 8th of October at eight o'clock in the evening I heard on the radio that the United Nations had formally approved the resolution in the full knowledge (which had been communicated to the State Department) that the Chinese would intervene in force.

I noted in my diary as follows:

"So, America has knowingly elected for war, with Britain following. It is indeed a tragic decision, for the Americans and the British are well aware that a military settlement of the Korean issue will be resisted by the Chinese and that the armies now concentrated on the Yalu border will intervene decisively in the fight. Probably that is what the Americans, at least some of them, want. They probably feel that this is the opportunity to have a showdown with China. In any case MacArthur's dream has come true. I only hope it does not turn out to be a nightmare. . . . Also I fear the Americans do not realize that they are fighting an armed revolution not only in China but all over Asia, in Indo-China, in Malaya, and in a lesser degree even in the Philippines, and the commission for the unification and rehabilitation of Korea which they have appointed, consisting among others of the Philippines, Siam, and Turkey, will never be able to do anything till the Chinese have been defeated."

On the ninth evening the Prime Minister transmitted to me a message from Ernest Bevin to be communicated personally to Chou En-lai. It was friendly in tone and contained vague assurances, including a promise that the Korean Commission would give the Chinese views their most careful consideration. Considering that the Commission consisted of countries like the Philippines and Siam, this promise looked to me like adding insult to injury. In any case Bevin's approach was too late, for the Chinese armies were already in Korea. Also the Chinese reacted most violently to the U.N. Resolution which a Foreign Office spokesman declared to be illegal.

By the middle of the month, there was no evidence that the Chinese had intervened. The Americans had occupied the northern capital of Pyongyang and were arranging to take over the entire territory. The Chinese soldiers had not been seen anywhere, and both in India and in America there was a measure of angry criticism directed against me personally. The American papers, even the most balanced ones like the *New York Herald Tribune*, began to say that I had been fooled and that Nehru was taken in by me. In India, a few pro-American papers echoed the criticism and there was even some demand that I should be recalled. MacArthur was hoping to conclude the campaign in triumph and had told the boys that they could go home by Christmas. I knew that the Chinese *had* intervened, but as there was no evidence of their fighting, my knowledge was of no importance. In the Indian Foreign Office also scepticism prevailed among the top officials. The Prime Minister alone was unmoved by all this agitation.

To add to my troubles, by the middle of the month, rumours of a Chinese invasion of Tibet began to circulate. Visits and representations to the Foreign Office brought no results. The Wai Chiaopu officials were polite but silent. Things were certainly moving on that side. The only information I was able to wring out of them was that certain pacificatory measures were being taken in West Sikang, that is on the borders of Tibet proper. In India, mainly as a result of messages from American and Hong Kong correspondents, public opinion was already excited. On the 25th of October, however, the Chinese announced on the Peking Radio that the process of "Liberating Tibet" had begun. The fat was in the fire. The Government of India was troubled about the Chinese action on the Tibetan borders and I received instructions to lodge a strong protest. The Chinese reply was equally strong. It practically accused India of having been influenced by the

Tibet

imperialists, and claimed that China had not taken any military action but was determined to liberate Tibet by peaceful means. Our rejoinder, though couched in equally strong words, recognized Chinese sovereignty over Tibet and disclaimed all desire to intervene in its affairs, and emphasized once again our desire that the issue between the Tibetans and the Chinese should be decided peacefully and not by the use of force. Both parties had made their point of view clear and were content to let it rest there.

I had expected a virulent campaign against India in the Press. But for some reason the Chinese, apart from publishing the correspondence, soft-pedalled the whole affair. The controversy was seldom mentioned in the Press. But on our side matters were not so easy. The Indian Press, egged on by the sensational reports of the American correspondents and the blood-curdling stories issued from Hong Kong by Taipeh agents, kept on talking about Chinese aggression. Even Sardar Patel, the Deputy Prime Minister, felt called upon to make an unfriendly speech. There was also some support in the External Affairs Ministry for the view that India should act vigorously to protect Tibet. In the meantime, Ecuador which was then a member of the Security Council, threatened to bring up the Tibetan question before the United Nations. Knowing the temper of the Indian public and the attitude of some of the officials I was nervous that the Government might take some hasty step. My own prestige with the Government was at a low ebb and I was being attacked for having misled the Prime Minister about Chinese intervention in Korea. But the Prime Minister was not so easily moved. He kept calm and allowed the public feeling to die down. In the meantime massive Chinese intervention in Korea had changed the entire situation.

At the beginning of November, driving out one day from my house, I saw a proclamation in red pasted everywhere on the walls in the usual Chinese way. It was being avidly read by passers-by including men in uniform. I returned home and sent out a servant to find out what it was about. It was a general appeal by all the parties to the Government Coalition emphasizing the necessity "to

H

aid Korea, resist America, defend the fatherland, protect the home." For the next few days public agitation against America was worked up to an unprecedented pitch. Everywhere, the walls were plastered with cartoons of Americans. It was a frightening display of bitterness and anger, and a deliberate effort to work up feelings and emotions against the Americans. A history of the American attitude towards China in the last century even pictured the Americans as inviting the Japanese to invade Manchuria. The volunteer army was publicly acclaimed as fighting for peace in Korea and for safe-guarding the Chinese Revolution.

Anyway, the intervention of China which upset the American plans and discredited the bellicose MacArthur came in time to re-establish my credit. The Prime Minister alone had stood by me and believed that the Chinese were not bluffing. The Tibetan question had also settled itself, for the Chinese after the first military display were content to keep their armies on the frontier and await the arrival of the Tibetan delegation for a settlement by negotiations. With the atmosphere thus cleared, I was in a position to take a little more active interest in the Korean affairs.

Realizing the importance of the Peking mission the Government sent T. N. Kaul, an experienced officer as counsellor. He reached Peking by the middle of November. He was in many ways an exceptional man. Though an I.C.S. officer of some seniority, he had as a result of his stay in Moscow and Washington shed the prejudices of "the heaven-born service" and had developed a genuinely progressive mind capable of appreciating the new forces in the world. He spoke Russian fairly fluently, and two years as first secretary in our embassy in Washington had given him an understanding of American psychology. He was a capable negotiator, friendly, firm, and shrewd. He had also a happy knack of maintaining contacts with different groups and at all levels. I was very happy to have him, especially because I was able to develop an informal line of contact with the Wai Chiaopu and with the Soviet *bloc*.

The situation in Korea in the meantime was rapidly deteriorating. The British Government was very unhappy, and Bevin wired to Hutchison a message to be conveyed to Chou En-lai or failing him to the highest accessible official. It was a strange communication, an elucidation of the objectives of the United Nations in Korea, an assurance from Britain that Chinese boundaries would be respected. There was a vague suggestion that there should be discussion with Chinese representatives at Lake Success. The Prime Minister wired to me to give full support to this representation, and when Hutchison discussed the matter with me I frankly told him that I doubted whether the Chinese would look at any proposal which did not include an offer of direct negotiations of the whole issue with them; and that I considered that the idea of Britain assuring China of the inviolability of her boundaries was patronizing, to say the least. The Chinese, who claimed to be able to ensure the inviolability of their own frontiers, would, I felt sure, consider the offer insulting as putting them in a category with the Philippines or Siam. I saw Chang Han-fu two days later and had an hour's talk with him. I strongly supported Bevin's proposal as offering an opening which the Chinese should take advantage of: the offer to discuss matters and the recognition of China's interest in Korea were two distinct gains. Though I put the arguments strongly I could not have sounded very convincing for the simple reason that I was not convinced myself.

Chang Han-fu was not greatly impressed by Bevin's proposals especially as they made no mention of Taiwan. To the Chinese, American action against Taiwan was no less important than the situation in Korea, though the western world was inclined to overlook the former as an embarrassing and inconvenient fact. The strange British idea of a neutralized zone, meaning thereby the annexation of the rest of Korea by Syngman Rhee, was naturally brushed aside as irrelevant by the Chinese.

Britain's approach to the Chinese issue suffered from a preliminary handicap. She could not bring herself to deal with China as an equal power. She was prepared to guarantee Chinese interests in Korea, to see that the so-called U.N. Committee on the unification of Korea took note of China's legitimate rights, etc., but she could not quite accept the idea that China should have at least as much voice as Britain and America in the settlement of issues in the Far East. All British proposals meant no more than that the Chinese should withdraw from Korea on British assurances and that America should be free to unify Korea under the cover of U.N. action.

The stiffness which had entered into our relations with China as a result of the Tibetan controversy had by this time totally disappeared. Slowly the relations began to improve. The Wai Chiaopu gave a dinner to Sen, my first secretary, who was going to Shanghai as Consul-General. At this the old theme of Sino-Indian friendship was again the subject of many toasts. To Kaul also they had been very friendly. Sen was among other things an excellent performer on an unusually sensitive instrument called Sarod and on the day before he left I persuaded him to give a private performance in my house. The Wai Chiaopu as usual selected the official Chinese guests. The list was fully representative of the cultural life of New China and included, besides Shen Ying-ping—the Minister of Culture—Chang Han-fu and his wife, Wang Ping-nan, Wang Jo-ju, the Director of the Central Musical Academy, Ma Tse-chung, Lu Chi, the composer, Madame Kuan, the famous soprano, Hung Tsien, the dramatist and writer and my old friends Hsu Pei-meng, the painter, and his wife. About half of the Chinese guests were non-communists. I showed some films relating to classical Indian dancing and this was followed by Sen's performance on the Sarod. The party went off in a most cordial and happy atmosphere, but I could not help feeling that it was strange that such a peace should reign in Peking when the whole world seemed to be frightened of developments in Korea.

It was the next morning (the 1st of December) that Truman announced that he was thinking of using the atom bomb in Korea. But the Chinese seemed totally unmoved by this threat. During the weeks that followed there were increased constructional activities along the city walls of Peking, widely believed to be preparations for underground cells against bombs of all kinds. Also, the propaganda against American aggression was stepped up. The "Aid Korea to resist America" campaign was made the slogan for increased production, greater national integration, and more rigid control over anti-national activities. One could not help feeling that Truman's threat came in very useful to the leaders of the revolution to enable them to keep up the tempo of their activities.

About this time I began to notice a change in the attitude of the westerners in Peking. In the early stages of the war, there was among them a great deal of suppressed satisfaction that China was now going to be taught a lesson. Over their interminable cock-tails they bewailed the disappearance of the China they knew and kept on hoping that a whiff of American bullets when America got down to it would dispose of the Chinese armies like chaff. The Military Attachés belonging to the old school had solemnly assured me before the American debacle that the Chinese troops could not stand up to the Americans as their training was in-adequate. The American defeat therefore came as a shock to them, and when Truman announced that he was thinking of dropping the atom bomb—most of them began smiling again. It was in this atmosphere that the West decided to celebrate St. Andrew's Day with all its accustomed gaiety. They still had the feeling that they were living in a European colony. I had gone in for a few minutes as Hutchison had pressed me, but the colonial atmosphere de-pressed me and I left early.

When the extent of American defeat became known I became very worried. My fear was that though the Americans might be dissuaded from dropping atom bombs, they might in desperation attack Manchuria and thereby extend the war. I was aware of the growing strength of China in the air: and the Chinese were certain that if Manchuria were attacked the Soviets would inter-vene. So with the authority of the Prime Minister, I approached the Chinese Government again (on the 8th of December) with the request that they should make a declaration that their forces would not move beyond the 38th parallel; that they would not move into South Korea. The line I took was that such a declaration would help to mobilize neutral opinion in China's favour and that they stood to lose nothing, as unless America agreed to respect that line China would also not be bound by her declaration. I also tried hard to prove to Chang Han-fu that it was foolish to think that a military decision was possible, for though the Americans might be forced back they could hold selected points on the coast as long as they had naval and air superiority. So the settlement had to be by negotiation, and now, as China had already shown her military strength, would it not be better, I argued, to offer to negotiate.

The thirteen (Asian-Arab) nations' appeal seemed to me to give an opening to the Chinese. At my suggestion Kaul saw Chen Chia-kang. Chen's reactions were interesting. He asked Kaul why the Philippines who were fighting in Korea had joined the thirteen nations. This was indeed strange, but it struck me as being even more strange when I heard Romulo denouncing Chinese aggression in Korea over the radio. Romulo, I then suspected, was probably preparing the ground for some new American action. In that case the Asian-Arab group, by keeping him with them, were only weakening their own position.

On the 11th of December Chou En-lai sent for me. We had an hour's conversation. The refrain of his talk was: "What do the Americans want? Do they want peace as we do, or are they going to persist in aggression? The Attlee–Truman communique clearly shows that what they want is war not peace." I replied that Government policies should not be judged from communiques but I was sure that Britain at least wanted peace and a Chinese declaration about the 38th parallel would help Britain and others who were trying to restrain the U.S.A. Chou En-lai replied, "So far as the 38th parallel is concerned, it is we, China and India, who wanted to uphold it. But MacArthur has demolished it and it exists no longer." I was altogether depressed after the interview for it was clear to me that the Chinese would not stop at the 38th parallel and the allies of America would be forced to trail behind in any action the U.S. proposed.

This sense of depression was increased by the news from America that Truman had declared a national emergency in the United States. All the talk was of mobilization, preparedness, etc., perhaps only to counteract the effect of defeat in Korea. Naturally it did not help the cause of peace. But all this shouting made no impression on the Chinese. They seemed to enjoy the reactions they were making on the Americans. I noted as follows in my diary:

"The strange thing is that neither the Soviets nor the Chinese have taken any public notice of these panicky actions. They go about their business as if nothing exceptional has happened and this lack of reaction is even more frightening than if they had blustered and threatened. The secrecy of the communist world gives you an uncanny feeling. Here in Peking there is an unnatural calm which is more deadly than all the shouting in America. . . . It has been announced in Washington that aeroplane production will be increased four and a half times and that 17,000 million dollars are to be spent this year on defence. No doubt it gives the ordinary American a feeling of satisfaction that everything *money* can do is being done to liquidate the communist menace. But the difficulty is that we do not know whether all this frightens the communists. Certainly it does not frighten the Chinese. The increase in the number of planes and in the weight of bombs seems to leave them cold, perhaps because they know that they have but few industries to be destroyed and equally they know that the bombs the Americans may make for a hundred years will not be sufficient to destroy the manpower of China."

The Arab-Asian group, which was ceaselessly active in the United Nations, had proposed two resolutions, the first for setting up a committee to negotiate a cease-fire and the second suggesting a conference for a peaceful settlement of the Far-Eastern issues. The proposal for the cease-fire as it stood was not altogether acceptable to the Americans. To the Chinese it appealed even less. Even so the Peking Government's reply went much farther than it need have. Chou En-lai not only refused to discuss anything with the committee but asserted that China did not accept as legal any resolution by the U.N. affecting her as long as she was not a party to the decision. After thus speaking for the record, Chou went on to state his terms: withdrawal from Taiwan, China's admission to U.N., withdrawal of all foreign troops from Korea, etc. Regarding the second proposal (for a Far-Eastern Conference) Chang Han-fu told me when I saw him (on Christmas Day) that the Chinese insisted on a prior acceptance in principle of their claim to Taiwan and for their seat in the U.N.

The commission of three, consisting of Rau, Lester Pearson, and Entezam, the Iranian President of the Assembly, put forward some new proposals, not very different from what had originally been proposed, except an acceptance in principle that all foreign troops should withdraw. These were sent on to me to be conveyed to the Chinese Government. My difficulty, which Mr. Nehru fully understood but Rau sitting in New York did not realize, was that I had no answer to the first question the Chinese were bound to ask: Have the proposals been approved by the American Government? In fact, while encouraging Rau and others to put forward proposals intended to draw out the Chinese, the Americans had all along refused to commit themselves. In the proposals which Rau had wired to me there was no mention of Taiwan, no proposals regarding the Korean settlement though the commission for this purpose, led by the Pakistanis, the Philippinos, and the Thailanders, was still in existence. The new proposals were to be incorporated in a report which was to be submitted by the committee to the U.N. and as such I asked the Chinese for no commitment but only for their reactions. Chang Han-fu's reply was simple. He asked whether they also represented the Government of India's own point of view. I had to parry that question by saying that the Government of India did not desire to formulate their views on these proposals without giving consideration to the Chinese reactions, and there the matter ended.

But things were moving fast. A day later I heard on the radio that the State Department had addressed all friendly States emphasizing the need to declare China an aggressor. The American note, it was reported, included also proposals that an economic blockade of China should be enforced, and that States which maintained diplomatic relations should withdraw their representatives. The reaction of those proposals on China was one more of amusement than of anger. China was not worried about being called an aggressor by the United States and her friends. So far as a blockade was concerned, the United States was already blockading her and the Chinese were satisfied that a publicly-declared blockade would help them to whip up enthusiasm for production and enable them to develop a "blockade economy," as the communists had previously done in Yenan. And as for the breaking-off of diplomatic relations, the Chinese knew well that none of the Asian countries would accept the American lead in the matter. So they looked upon these proposals as another evidence of American hysteria.

It was fortunate that the Commonwealth Premiers' conference was then meeting in London. The American proposals were unlikely to be viewed sympathetically there. Actually on the 12th of January, 1951, I received a telegram from Prime Minister Nehru sent from London suggesting a new conference on Korea without anything tacked to it like the old suggestion of de-militarized zones. As it happened, when the telegram arrived, we were dining at Kaul's house with Chiao Kan-hua, the Vice-Chairman of the Policy Committee of the Foreign Office, and Chen Chia-kang, the Director of Asian Affairs. Their reaction seemed favourable and it appeared to me that on those lines we could get a move forward. Unfortunately the optimism of the previous night cooled down during the day when the radio announced that the original Commonwealth proposals had been modified by the inclusion of the provision for a cease-fire prior to the negotiations. I was able to meet Chang Han-fu the same evening at a private dinner given by Shen Ying-ping, the Minister of Culture. He explained to me that the original proposals might have provided a basis, but the insistence on a prior cease-fire was an insuperable difficulty. I strongly advised Chang Han-fu not to reject the proposals on that ground but to accept what was suitable and either ask for modifications or make counter proposals in regard to others.

On the 15th I saw Chang Han-fu officially and gave him the substance of the Prime Minister's telegram conveying the Commonwealth Prime Ministers' views. I had made an analysis of the proposal and stated in a tabular form the differences between the previous proposals and the present one, with the object of convincing the Chinese how their interests had been safeguarded. My final stand was: If you are not satisfied with my elucidations why not ask the political committee for elucidation or, better still, proceed on the assumption that your interpretation is correct and leave it to the other party either to reject or to explain the matter further.

I was taking a very considerable risk in interpreting the text on my own and offering elucidations which no one had authorized me to do. Directly and through Kaul I had been raining unofficial memoranda and notes on the Wai Chiaopu, because apart from my desire to get the proposals through on their merits, I realized that Pandit Nehru's authority and prestige were committed at least to a modified acceptance of these proposals. So interpreting his mind to the best of my ability, but without any express directions from him, I did not hesitate to tell the Chinese that the explanations I was giving were in conformity with the Prime Minister's own views. In view of the urgency of the question and the difficulty of getting instructions from Nehru who was spending the week-end at Chequers I had no other option.

But I confess I was greatly relieved when on the 16th of January I received from Pandit Nehru a detailed appraisal of the situation which in many places agreed word for word with the analysis which I had on my own passed on to the Chinese. I felt that my hands had been greatly strengthened and immediately sent Kaul to Chen with instructions to read out relevant extracts to him. Kaul, whose personal relations with the Director were excellent, spent an hour with him and came back firmly convinced that there would be no rejection of the proposals. I was, however, not satisfied with this. Early next morning I sent with Kaul unofficially to Chen Chia-kang a paraphrased version of the Prime Minister's telegram, for I knew the Cabinet was in session and I wanted the paper to reach Chou En-lai at the meeting before a decision was finally reached by him and his colleagues. At seven o'clock in the evening I received an intimation that Chou En-lai would see me at nine o'clock. I cannot remember any occasion in my whole life when I was so excited. I knew that much depended on the nature of the Chinese reply. If China rejected the proposals the United States would undoubtedly be able to organize world opinion against her. If on the other hand the Chinese accepted the principle of settlement by negotiation and made alternative proposals the edge of the U.S.A.'s efforts to mobilize the world against China would be blunted and peace would be saved. It was to this end the Prime Minister had worked and had secured the support of the Commonwealth Nations behind the proposals. A rejection of the proposals would be a defeat for him.

Realizing the importance of the occasion I took Kaul with me and we arrived at the Wai Chiaopu at nine o'clock punctually. Chou En-lai had not yet arrived at the office and we were received by Chen Chia-kang. Though we were bursting to ask him what the decision was, my sense of diplomatic propriety was strong enough to overcome my curiosity and the conversation turned round the greatness of the Himalayas, the common mountain range which separated India and China. Chou En-lai entered the room at 9.15 accompanied by his interpreter and Chaio Kan-hua. From the first moment it was clear that there was going to be no rejection. During the conversation which extended for over an hour he paid great tributes to Pandit Nehru and handsome compliments to myself, adding that he had studied with care and attention the numerous notes and memoranda I had sent to him.

Though the Chinese reply was a qualified acceptance, with alternative proposals in respect of points which they did not accept, the Americans even before they had time to study it declared that it was "a contemptuous rejection" and immediately brought up proposals to brand China as "an aggressor." The reason for this strange action became clear later, when Ambassador Grosse frankly confessed before the Senate that America had accepted the original proposals only because she thought that China would reject them. The fact that China did not reject them upset their plans and they had therefore to carry on as if the Chinese reply was a rejection. Nehru wired for some further elucidation on points raised by St. Laurent and these were also supplied. St. Laurent had asked that the reply should reach him before Monday afternoon, and as the difference in time did not permit me to use the normal channels I decided to send the Chinese reply *en clair* to Rau at Lake Success with a request to hand it over to Lester Pearson.

My arrangements worked to perfection. The telegram conveying the Chinese Government's elucidations arrived just before the

American resolution was to be put to the vote, and when Rau read my message it created a sensation. The American delegates were so upset that the only thing they could think of as an answer was to say that as these elucidations were given to India and not to the United Nations, no notice should be taken of them and the committee should go forward and vote as if nothing had happened. Such a line of action could have been only the result of confusion. The adjournment of forty-eight hours which was proposed by Rau in order to enable the delegations to study the elucidations was vehemently opposed by the Americans but it was carried by twenty-seven to twenty-three. I knew, however, that this was only a momentary victory: that the Americans would use the whip mercilessly and line up their friends to get China declared an aggressor. But the sting had gone from the resolution. Even the people who voted for that resolution knew that they were only saving America's face. This became clear when America proposed the additional measures resolution, which had to be watered down to such an extent that it became practically use-less. Even the "branding" resolution when it was passed had a rider attached to it, no doubt to salve the British conscience, that no sanctions would be applied till all avenues of peace had been explored. The United Nations also appointed a committee of three to keep in touch with the Chinese Government and to work to bring about peace. But the Chinese had made it amply clear that there would be no political negotiations with the U.N. as long as the "illegal" resolution branding them as aggressors remained on the record.

Thus ended the first major effort to bring about a settlement in Korea. Perhaps the time had not come; in any case the American Government was, in view of mounting hostility to China in the public mind, unable at that time to accept any proposals for peace. They had not got over the unpleasant surprise of military defeat and to have accepted a cease-fire then would have left the impres-sion that they were accepting terms under the weight of military defeat. Another year had to pass before the matter could be taken up again.

CHAPTER X

LIFE IN PEKING. II

ON the 26th of January, 1951, we celebrated the first anniversary of the Indian Republic. I gave a dinner reception at the Peking Hotel and everyone was surprised when Mao Tse-tung himself attended the function and proposed the main toast. For weeks foreign papers had been publishing news of Mao's illness, asserting that he had been deposed by Liu Shao-chi. Many other canards of a similar character had found currency in foreign papers. The Hong Kong journals, which under Taipeh inspiration excelled in this kind of propaganda, had persuaded most western diplomatists that something was wrong with Mao Tse-tung. So when Mao arrived at any party, it created something of a sensation among them. But more was to come. Mao Tse-tung proposed the toast of India in a short speech. He began by saying "It is a great day. The Indian people are a fine people. There have been thousands of years of friendship between the people of India and China." It was a genuine, simple utterance pronounced slowly in short sentences, but it had a great effect on everyone who heard him. During our conversation at dinner Mao Tse-tung displayed much interest in the development of good relations with India. He spoke in warm terms about Nehru and said that he hoped to be able to see him soon in China. He talked about the exchange of students and professors, about learning each other's language, about his desire to see an Indian film depicting the life of the ordinary people. His conversation in fact left with me an impression of the deep human interest which Mao has in his fellow beings.

My only sorrow during these months was the condition of my wife's health. The severity of the Peking winter had been too much for her frail body and she was seriously ill for over four months. Her life was almost despaired of, but the devoted attention of Colonel Bertrand of the French hospital pulled her through. But the doctor was firm that she should not spend another winter in China and warned that, if she did, it might prove fatal. So during all the difficult days of November, December and January when I had to carry on the most delicate negotiations, I had this heavy load on my mind. But the beautiful spring of Peking did wonders and by the middle of April she was again in reasonably good health. Dr. Bertrand had returned to France and at the suggestion of General Roschin, the Soviet Ambassador, I entrusted her treatment to the Russian specialists then in Peking. A remarkable team of Soviet doctors had been engaged by the Chinese Government for the reorganization of their hospitals in Peking. They included specialists in every line, and I am very grateful to them for taking a special interest in the treatment of my wife.

Early in February (1951) some information reached me about the activities of a strange organization named Yi Kuan-tao. There were rumours of large-scale Government action against this body, on the ground of encouraging superstition which worked for reaction and on account of rumour-mongering. The original organization of Yi Kuan-tao seems to have been started in 1913 immediately after the fall of the Manchus. Its founder, Lu Chung-yi, who had proclaimed himself an incarnation of the Buddha, started it as a religious sect. On his death in 1923, his sister succeeded him and converted it into a small church with local priests who collected funds for her and sold charms in her name. Its following was mainly among rickshaw coolies, hawkers, porters, etc. Under her successor, Chang Kuan-pi, who took the title of Respected Sage, the organization became something of a secret society and spread to different parts of China. He established lodges in different places and became a powerful figure in the internal politics of China. He was undoubtedly used by the Japanese as one of their agents. After the Japanese war the Kuomintang also found the Yi Kuan-tao useful. The Respected Sage died at Chengtu in 1947 and was succeeded as the Grand Master of the Order by his wife Sun Su-chen.

The public organization of the sect was somewhat as follows: There were "Churches" or lodges in all the important cities and under these were branch and family rostrums each with a Director, Vice-Director, Priest and San Tsai, the initiator. The words of God, revealed through the planchets, were drawn by the initiates. Those initiated had of course to take a solemn oath and pay a "merit fee." When you paid the fee you were given the three treasures, Chueh, Kuan and Yin. The Chueh were five secret charms or spells ensuring long life, physical potency, happiness, etc. Kuan was the communication of the holy spirit by the priest, which gave you special qualities and made you the favoured of God. Yuan was the manner of worship. All this was of course secret.

The priests of this strange sect knew the value of mystifying rituals and they had by these methods come to acquire great power over a section of the ignorant masses. The Kuomintang authorities seemed to have considered them as useful channels of propaganda, and in any case they became their agents for spreading the most absurd rumours among the people. For many months I had been hearing stories of strange prophesies circulating among the people, excitement among servants about supernatural manifestations, etc. Then one day it was mentioned to me by a friend that in the Central Park there were crowds witnessing some kind of extraordinary performance which had been taking place under official auspices during the past few days. I sent my third secretary, Dr. Virendra Kumar, who spoke Chinese fluently, to go and see it. He reported in the evening that it was nothing less than the public confession of the Grand Master and High Priests of the Yi Kuan-tao, accompanied by a public performance of their secret rites, humbly explaining to the public the charlatanry they practised on the people.

What the Central People's Government did when they decided to liquidate the Yi Kuan-tao was to arrest the Grand Master and the high priests and to announce to the members that the "merit fee" exacted from them would be returned to them, if they surrendered their charms and spells. But knowing that superstition dies hard, the Government also decided to expose the tricks and charlatanries of the sect. The Grand Master and the high priests were asked to conduct the ceremonies and to explain to the people

the trickeries they practised. They were then made to apologize
for the fraud they committed on the public. This went on for
weeks, making the Yi Kuan-tao a source of public amusement.

Apart from legal action against old-time gangs like the Yellow
Ox and the secret societies with which China was riddled, it
became clear by about the end of March that the Government was
planning action on a mass scale against "counter-revolutionaries."
On the 26th of March no less than 199 counter-revolutionaries were
executed in Peking. After that, I gathered from various sources
that all over the country martial law courts had been set up to deal
with the problem of the remnants of the Kuomintang which had
been left behind to form the nucleus of resistance and rebellion
when Chiang Kai-shek returned to the mainland. There was no
doubt some reason for the People's Government to take strong
measures to destroy the effectiveness of this underground force.
It was frequently stated that plans had been worked out by the
American Intelligence Officers (General Donovan's name was
frequently mentioned) in co-operation with the exiles in Taiwan
to make some landings in the south. Both the Americans and the
Kuomintang believed that the south was ready to rise against
Peking and there were many comings and goings between
Tokyo and Taipeh, and announcements from Taiwan of impend-
ing invasions. The Peking authorities were in no mood to take risks,
and the mass campaign they started for the liquidation of counter-
revolutionaries and reactionary elements seems to have effectively
disposed of over a million and a half people who were either
actively Kuomintang agents or suspected of sympathies with
Taipeh.

What worried me more than the "liquidation" of the counter-
revolutionaries which was in some ways only a continuation of the
civil war, was the policy which the Government was pursuing
towards the missionaries, nuns and Christian priests of foreign
nationality. All my life I have been an opponent of missionary
activity in the East. I have always considered the missionaries as
spiritually arrogant, contemptuous of the faiths and beliefs of
others, subversive in their social purposes and propagandists for
the theory of the inherent superiority of Europe. China, especially

had a clear and unanswerable case against the missionaries, for mission work in the country had been under the protection of extra-territoriality. But for all that, I could not understand the policy of the Government in regard to European missionaries. Those who desired to go away could not get exit visas. Their lives were rendered altogether miserable. Charges of the most extraordinary kind were made against them by the public. Catholic nuns in different cities were accused and tried of large-scale murder of children in their orphanages. The circumstances of trial were also by no means pleasing. The proceedings were broadcast. There was nothing very much I could do, but both from the point of view of humanity and as a friend of China interested in her good name I took up the matter more than once with Chou En-lai. In this work I had the staunch support of the Swiss Minister, Clement Rezzonico, who was a man of great sensibility and exceptional understanding. Though an ardent catholic, and a conservative, he had sufficient sympathy for New China to understand, if not appreciate, the changed attitude of Peking towards the West. We therefore worked hand in hand to secure some amelioration of the conditions of the missionaries. In my conversations with Chou En-lai on this question I always emphasized that China would not lose anything by allowing the missionaries to go away by giving them exit permits freely. I never got a really satisfactory answer about this matter. The only case in which I could claim some success was that of Archbishop Riberi, who was Internuncio in Nanking when I was there. When the communists took over he stayed on in his capacity as Apostolic Delegate. His position was a very difficult one. The attitude of the Vatican towards communism, based both on ideological grounds and on the treatment accorded to the Catholic Church in such countries as Poland and Hungary, traditionally devoted to the Holy See, was one of uncompromising hostility. Catholics formed the most important section of the Chinese Christian community and it was the Archbishop's function to hold them to their faith, to help and encourage them to resist the attempts that were then being made to establish a national Catholic Church. Through the Legion of Mary and other organizations he worked hard to this end, thereby providing justification for the Chinese charge that he, the agent of a foreign State, was interfering in the affairs of China. The Archbishop was arrested and interrogated. At this stage I felt that it might be useful to mention the matter to Chou En-lai. I put it to him, on purely personal grounds, that the Archbishop had been my colleague in Nanking and was my friend; that I entertained a high opinion of his character and integrity and therefore I would like him to be sent out of China rather than be imprisoned for subversive activity. Chou En-lai did not say anything, but a few days later when the Archbishop was actually sent out of China I felt that perhaps I had been able to do something on behalf of my friend. Very soon afterwards, I received through Rezzonico a message of thanks from the Holy See.

Rezzonico and myself set ourselves up as an unofficial two-man committee to assist the nationals of countries not represented in Peking—Italy, France, Belgium, etc.—to get their exit visas, and to make normal enquiries about their conditions if they were interned in jail. I do not think we had much success but we kept on persistently urging our point of view and using every opportunity available to us to press the matter home.

The general flow of life in Peking at this time was not unpleasant. What the communists call "cultural life" was being actively encouraged. In the international club there were regular musical evenings at which Chinese artistes performed occasional ballets and other performances. What I liked best was the Peking Opera. The communists while keeping the old forms have of course changed the content of the pieces, and the favourites are no longer old stories from *The Three Kingdoms*, *The Oilman and the Dancing Girl*, or plays of a romantic character, but those with themes relating to the class struggle, such as the famous opera *The White-Haired Girl*. Actually it was not much more than the use of a venerable and very popular art form for propaganda purposes; but there was no denying the fact that it was extremely effective and of high artistic quality. The old artificialities of the Peking Opera have been simplified, but the archaic manner has been preserved. In *The White-Haired Girl* the tension of modern drama and the fine acting by the chief characters enable one to overlook the crudities of its politics.

One of the most interesting performances I witnessed was by the celebrated female impersonator Mei Lan-fang in a play entitled *The Legend of the Peony Pavilion*. The first time I saw Mei Lan-fang act it almost took my breath away. Mei was then fifty-six but he was acting the part of a girl of twenty. The acting was so convincing that till I was told that it was a man who was acting and that he was over fifty-five I was under the impression that Mei Lan-fang was a young woman! I remember Ellen Terry, then past sixty, acting the part of Portia at the Shakespeare Tercentenary Festival in 1917. But it was a strained performance. Anyone could see that the old lady was trying desperately to recapture a vanished atmosphere. In Mei Lan-fang's case there was no such straining for effect. He acted naturally and seemed to have a young woman's soul.

The piece was a Kun Opera of the Ming period. The story is very thin and very simple. A young lady goes for a walk in the garden accompanied by her maid. It is spring time and her fancy naturally turns to love. There is some good singing and dancing in the garden in appreciation of spring-time beauty. Returning to her boudoir, the heroine falls asleep and in her dream she meets her love and they go off for a stroll along hills and dales. When she wakes up after her romance she is roundly scolded by her mother for being a lazy good-for-nothing. The story gives ample opportunity for romantic acting, dancing, and singing, in all of which Mei Lan-fang is a master. Afterwards I have had many opportunities of seeing him act in many different pieces including one which I was told he has composed himself in honour of the goodwill mission led by Mrs. Pandit, and always I felt the same thrill as when I saw him first.

The Chinese restaurants of Peking were of course a perpetual source of joy. In a spirit of adventure we wandered all over Peking in search of them. A young Chinese lady by the name of Christine Kung who was a great friend of my daughter used to accompany us on these expeditions. We used to select restaurants with provincial specialities and were amply repaid for the trouble we took by the rare quality of the food which these out-of-the-way restaurants served. The most interesting and perhaps the most famous of these places is the Mongolian restaurant near the Bell Tower. It is an amazing place, a broken-down hut in a narrow street among malodorous surroundings. It faces one of the extensions of the Peihai lake. There were but three small rooms and the bitter north wind kept coming through uncovered patches in the roof. But the place itself was scrupulously clean. In the central room was a big oven where the customer cooked his own meat. The attendants prepared the meat—the famous Mongolian mutton—washed it and brought it up to you on a plate. You did the rest. You mixed it up with sauce and some greens and put the whole on the surface of the pan which was shaped like the back of a tortoise. A blazing fire continuously burnt under this pan. There, with your chopsticks, you kept turning the meat till it became properly cooked. Then you transferred the meat into a bowl in which you had already prepared a sauce of beaten eggs and sugar. You ate standing near the oven and when one bowl was over you began cooking another.

The most interesting experience I had in this restaurant was with Rewe Alley, the famous New Zealander who had been the life and soul of "Indusco," the industrial co-operatives about which we used to hear so much during the Sino-Japanese war. He is now running the Santan school where he is attempting to introduce into Chinese rural life scientific skills and methods, meant to change the productive system of the villages. Rewe Alley is a broad-built, pleasant-looking man with a fine sense of humour and generous sentiments. Talking to him, one would hardly think that he has been living and teaching in out-of-the-way places in the interior of China for over fifteen years—a new and strange kind of missionary. Rewe Alley, who makes no secret now of being a communist, told me that he was saved from facing a Kuomintang firing squad by the good opinion that Sir Ralph Stevenson formed of him and his work.

The party where I met Rewe Alley was given by Dr. Atal who had led the Indian Medical Mission to China in 1937. Others invited were Burchett, the Australian newspaper correspondent, and a Syrian doctor (Chinese name Ma Hai-tai), married to a Chinese film star. Burchett was a cocksure advocate of peace, who gave the impression that he felt convinced that he was saving the world by shouting the slogans of the peace congress. Ma Hai-tai, who had spent nineteen years of his life in America, has been working with the Chinese communists for the last twelve years. He was one of the original group of foreigners in Yenan and had stayed on in China, securing employment in the Public Health Ministry. His Chinese wife was a cinema actress of unusual beauty, who looked more like a countess from a convent school. Her conversation was interesting and intelligent and she seemed to be wide awake about world affairs.

Both Rewe Alley and Ma Hai-tai were mighty eaters and, as if in competition, they stood near the oven and cooked and ate no less than twelve dishes of meat—a record I should think even at this Mongolian restaurant. The conversation ranged from American propaganda to Chinese names, and as three of them, Atal, Rewe Alley and Ma Hai-tai had been at Yenan, we heard a great deal of reminiscences about that legendary period when Mao Tse-tung and his associates were living in caves and directing a guerrilla warfare all over China.

Political activity in relation to the Korean peace had come more or less to a standstill with the branding of China as an aggressor, but when MacArthur was dismissed there was a slight flutter of activity. On the 11th of April at 7 p.m. I heard over the B.B.C. that Truman had deprived MacArthur of all his commands. No longer the S.C.A.P., no longer the Supreme Commander of the United Nations Forces, no longer the super-Mikado, the man who thought he could defy anybody and get away with it found himself like a recalcitrant priest unfrocked by superior authority. Strange is the power of democracy. The most powerful soldier, in command of vast forces and exercising for the time supreme control over a great Empire, is dismissed by a simple order, and he has no option but to surrender his authority and leave. The world looked up in pleased surprise. But the Chinese, strangely enough, showed no interest in the matter. For four days there was no comment in the Chinese papers about MacArthur's dismissal.

Finally on the 15th we had a plethora of articles, all meaning the same thing: MacArthur has been recalled because he was defeated: because Truman wanted to put the blame on him for the failure of the Americans in Korea. On careful consideration, I had myself come to the conclusion that the fall of MacArthur would not immediately improve the chances of peace. The political situation in the U.S.A. following MacArthur's dismissal would make it difficult for Truman to talk of peace, for the Republicans, I calculated, would lose no opportunity to capitalize on the President's action.

The Government of India kept on pressing me to take advantage of the new situation created by the dismissal of MacArthur. But my feeling was that the situation had not changed materially, that Truman had only denounced MacArthur's "deviationism"—his tendency to play off his own bat—that American policy both in respect of Taiwan and of the Peking Government's recognition remained unchanged. I saw Chang Han-fu all the same, and pressed for some friendly gesture, but he was most unresponsive. So I retired into my shell.

At this time we were negotiating for a grain deal with China, for milo and rice, a matter which caused some astonishment to western nations, who had been continuously fed on propaganda about "famine conditions" in China. Hong Kong had been putting out stories of large-scale scarcity conditions in different parts of China as a result of communist oppression, and the offer to sell foodgrains to India had not, therefore, been taken seriously by the West. But when the agreement was signed and the ships began loading in Darein, they changed their tune. The American papers declared that it was a political deal, that China was depriving herself of food to make an impression on India. Anyway, I was happy that when food conditions in India were serious and we were facing famine China was able to sell us the grain we required so urgently.

When the winter was over, I suggested to the Wai Chiaopu that facilities should be afforded me to visit villages in different parts of China in order to understand the effects of the land reform policy about which one had heard so much. The Chinese Govern-

ment made no difficulty. The first villages selected lay some miles
to the north of the Marcopolo bridge. We were accompanied by
two members of the peasants' association and an officer from the
protocol. Till we reached the Marcopolo bridge—the scene of the
famous Sino-Japanese incident—there was nothing very special one
could see, except evidences of renewed building activity, repairs
of canals, etc. Crossing the bridge, which was heavily guarded at
both ends, we came to a ridge, a natural defensive barrier, something like the Delhi Ridge, where we saw a great deal of military
preparation. There were light tanks and other army vehicles
parked against the hill-side—partly no doubt as protection against
bandits, but partly also as a precaution against airborne landings
meant to disrupt military communications with the north. Also,
there were small factories, dotted all over the landscape, eviden-
cing an intensive activity in this field. We reached the village, the
name of which I forget now, at about 12.15. As this was the first
village in communist China that I visited—though I had occasion
during the course of the year to see scores more in different parts
of the country—a short description of the visit and the impressions I gathered may be of interest.

We were met on arrival by the Chairman, Vice-Chairman, and
members of the village committee and escorted courteously to the
village school. The committee is elected by all the adult population
of the village—excluding of course the dispossessed landowners.
Previously the committee members had all been either landless
labourers or poor farmers (that is owning less than an acre and
cultivating it by their own labour). As soon as we were seated and
treated to the customary cups of tea, I began asking questions
through my own interpreter Dr. Kumar. How many mows of
land did the Chairman have before? How much has he now? How
many cattle, farm implements? How much did he make out of the
land? What did he give to the State? What was his net income?
How did he propose to spend it? The Vice-Chairman who was an
intelligent young farmer acted as the spokesman and gave full
and frank replies. There were no extravagant claims. The production figures which he quoted were not very different from those
in normal areas in India. What interested me most was the new

spirit. The members of the committee, though poor or landless peasants, had a full appreciation of what had been done and were talking to me as free and independent men. They discussed the issues which I had raised with a clear understanding of how they affected local conditions. For example, when I asked the committee about the prospects of co-operative farming, the question rather worried them; but when Kumar explained what I meant, they all shouted together: "Yes, of course, this is exactly what we have been discussing among ourselves. We are trying to work out a scheme of labour pool and common marketing."

I went round the school which had eight teachers and 250 students. Though a primary school, some of the students were quite grown up, as they were having an opportunity to go to school for the first time. Afterwards we walked round the fields, inspecting a number of plots, each cultivated by the owner by his own and his family's labour. One of the peasants explained to me the cropping system. I have considerable experience of inspecting cultivated lands since this is an unavoidable duty for the Prime Minister of an Indian State. Apart from that, I myself came from farming stock and had some direct knowledge of similar conditions in India. I was therefore able to enter into discussions with them about the technical aspects of their problems. When they discovered my interest they became quite expansive and explained to me how they got over minor difficulties, how the peasant association brought to them the experience of other villages, etc. etc.

Seeing a large and imposing building at the far end of the village I asked what it was. A temple, I was told. What was it used for now? "An orphanage and an old people's house maintained by the village," was the reply. Passing the temple, we came to the co-operative store. It was well stocked with consumer goods and also with bean cakes for manure. But what attracted my attention most was a well-displayed document hanging on the wall—the Patriotic Testament, which all the members of the co-operative society had signed. Apart from the slogans of fighting American aggression, helping Korea, defending the fatherland, it pledged members to work for increased production, to safeguard people's property (public assets), to understand politics better, etc. This Patriotic Testament—a kind of covenant signed by the people—was one of the most effective methods of national integration that the new regime had introduced, and later during my travels I was able to see how far it had penetrated, into the desert area of Gobi no less than into the best rice villages of Canton.

After this, I went in, on my own, into a worker's house. It was a one-room tenement of mud and plaster—newly built by the owner himself. He was a landless worker before, and when the plot was allotted to him he built the house himself. It was a clean, spacious room but there was in it a beautiful vase—a sign to me of inherent culture. The owner was not there when I went in but he came back in a hurry, his hands dirty with mud as he was working. He shook hands with me most vigorously, forgetting the mud on his hands, and insisted on my taking the usual tea. The only other house I saw in the village was one in which an old widow, the mother of a P.L.A. man, was living. It was also a one-room house. On the *kang* or the Chinese built-in bed were four large boxes. At least two of them, it seemed to me from their appearance, she must have received when the landlord's superfluous property was distributed. There were also a number of vases, a clock, a photograph of the hero-son, and lots of chickens in the courtyard. The old widow received me in the manner of a duchess, with great condescension; was not her son a hero, fighting perhaps in Korea?—and she insisted on being photographed with me.

The main impression I had of the village was one of freedom, of an immense release of energy, of a great spirit of self-assurance and desire to achieve things. Economically a holding of three mow (three-fifths of an acre) for an individual is nothing very much. But the land reform has broken the chains, made the villager free, and has given him a new sense of dignity and self-respect. That is indeed a great achievement.

In May we had an unofficial goodwill mission from India, the first of many to be exchanged between China and India. Though it was an unofficial one, and some of its members were connected with front organizations, I had actively encouraged this visit as I felt that I would be able to handle the delegation, many of whom I had known quite well for many years. The leader of the delegation was Pandit Sunderlal, a man of very good impulses and high character, but a little uncritical and inclined to be over-enthusiastic. But the delegation also contained men like Dr. V. K. R. V. Rao, the Director of the Delhi School of Economics, Prof. Mahommed Habib who had been with me at Oxford and had succeeded me as Professor at Aligarh where he still held the Chair of History, Prof. Mujeeb, his brother, head of the Jamia Millia and Mrs. Hannah Sen, the President of the All-India Women's Conference, none of whom could be accused of fellow-travelling or pro-communist politics. Leftist opinion was also amply represented in the delegation by Mulk Raj Anand whom I had known from his college days in London, and by Karanjia, the vivacious editor of *Blitz*, whose private social behaviour and general understanding of issues bore no relation to his public face as the editor of the sensational weekly. I had only a casual acquaintance with Karanjia before his arrival in China and the *Blitz* had not prejudiced me in his favour. But in Peking I came to know him better, and though I cannot praise the methods of journalism which he has practised so successfully in Bombay, I came to like him as a man, and as one who had an appreciation of some of the essential issues of politics.

The Chinese Foreign Office was not quite certain how I would react to the visit of this unofficial delegation but I assured them when they raised the matter with me that I was quite happy with the selection of the personnel of the delegation and anticipated no difficulties with them. I went personally to the airport to welcome them; and when the Chinese leaders who had gathered there saw Sunderlal, on getting down from the plane, embrace me cordially as a long-lost brother, they were quite surprised. On the very next day the delegates came to me for a briefing and for over four hours they discussed all issues frankly with me. The Chinese authorities realized that the relations of the Indian Government even with those who opposed them were not of the kind which they had imagined, and as a result everything went off very well. At the banquet given in their honour the embassy was fully represented, and Pandit Sunderlal's speech followed mainly the lines of my own public utterances, though it was more effusive and less restrained. The mission visited different parts of China and were treated with the greatest friendliness.

I was looking forward to witnessing the May Day celebrations, my first in Peking. It was ideal weather, and at 9.30 the diplomatic corps took its stand on the gallery erected for them. Punctually at ten, Mao Tse-tung showed himself on the balcony, and immediately an immense procession carrying banners, huge portraits of the leaders of the proletariat of all countries, and cartoons of American action, began to march past. There were many thousands of bright red silk banners and flags. Every conceivable device had been used to make the procession attractive and picturesque from front, from above, and from the sides; for instance one group marched in a square formation, all red on the top with five stars in yellow, which if viewed from the air would look like an immense flag.

Seven hundred thousand men, women, boys, and girls, marched past in six hours. Mao Tse-tung stood there on the balcony of the Tien An Men—the gate of Heavenly Peace—from ten o'clock to 3.15 without once sitting down or relaxing, though all of us in the diplomatic gallery retired from time to time to rest a little. For over two months the Hong Kong papers had been talking about Mao's illness, about his being put on the shelf by the Russians. In fact many among the western diplomats even in Peking had begun to believe that Mao was seriously ill, as he had not appeared at any public function after the Indian National day on the 26th of January. But there on the balcony he had stood like a rock for five hours and a quarter, waving his hands every two minutes. The Swedish Ambassador, Hammustrom, insisted that it could not be Mao but his double and repeated many stories of Hitler's days to prove his point. Moerch, the Danish Minister, was equally convinced that Mao had been artificially propped up, and that he must have had numerous injections before coming to the ceremony. This was what the West liked to believe.

Since the end of January I had not seriously interested myself in the Korean situation, feeling that it would be best to lie low till both sides were in a better mood. All suggestions from Delhi for

taking up again the thread of negotiations were discouraged by
me, and the Prime Minister who fully understood the position did
not also press the matter any further. But early in May, B. N. Rau
wired from New York that the Little Assembly was likely to
recommend "sanctions" against China unless the conference idea
could be renewed. It did not appear to me that a conference
under U.N. auspices was likely to appeal to the Chinese and I
replied to Rau in that sense. But on reconsideration, I thought
that there might be a new opening for peace talks if Rau could
put forward a proposal for a conference outside the United
Nations—that is, one convened by Britain or Russia or even India
and confined to the powers interested in the Far East. Nothing
came out of this for the moment and on the 16th the American
proposal for an embargo on China was passed by the political
committee. The Indonesian chargé, Izzak Mahdi, made the most
interesting comment on it. The embargo would not hurt the
Chinese much, but it would hurt Indonesia since the Americans
would be able to force down the price of rubber in the absence
of Chinese purchasers!

Though I was despondent about the immediate possibility of
bringing about a truce in Korea, I kept myself in close touch with
my colleagues of the Soviet *bloc*, especially with Burgin, the
Polish Ambassador, who was always prepared to discuss questions
reasonably, as well as with Wezikopf whose attitude to the entire
Far-Eastern problem I found extremely interesting. Burgin had
visited North Korea and what he told me of conditions there was
almost unbelievable. According to him over eighty-five per cent
of the houses in North Korea had been destroyed and Pyongyang
was a city of ruins and the people were living in holes and caves:
but the morale of the North Koreans was high and their fighting
spirit was higher than ever. This had been told me by others also;
people who had been to Korea and come back. I was therefore
satisfied that there was no possibility of the Americans gaining a
military decision, especially as the Chinese air force had become a
factor of importance.

In the meantime, I had developed a new interest. On the 30th
of April, Mr. Hoang, who was the head of the Vietnam delegation

in Peking, with the rank of ambassador, asked me for an interview.
India's position in regard to the two rival States in Vietnam has
been one of strict neutrality. We had refused to accept either the
Bao Dai regime which had been sponsored by the French, or
Ho Chi Minh's Government which had been recognized by the
Chinese as being the sole Government of Annam; and our declared
attitude was that we should recognize as the Government of
Vietnam only the party which had control at least of the major
portion of the State. The fact that Bao Dai was a French nominee
and was kept on his precarious throne by French bayonets made it
wholly impossible for us to recognize him as an independent ruler.
So far as Ho Chi Minh was concerned, though his Government
controlled large areas he was still fighting for victory and had not
established his authority over the entire State. So while the
sympathy of the people of India was, generally speaking, on the
side of the national freedom movement, we had been careful to
maintain an attitude of strict neutrality. Hoang's request, however,
did not embarrass me. I was desirous of meeting him so that I
could develop some kind of contact with what had undoubtedly
become one of the major facts of Asian politics—the growth of a
new democratic State in Indo-China.

Hoang was a youngish man who spoke French fluently but no
English; but his First Secretary, a young man of great ability, knew
India well and spoke excellent English. Hoang had been a guerrilla
fighter for many years and was intimate with Ho Chi Minh and
other leaders who control the movement. His view, which he
explained to me at some length, was that Vietminh had already
won "the basic victory" as was proved by the fact that during the
last five years France had been unable to take the offensive. So far
as his Government was concerned, it was in no hurry to take
over the cities till it had established itself, had fully organized
the territory under its control, and had developed its own cadres
and worked out a new economic policy, all of which he indicated
they were doing systematically in the area now occupied by them.
I asked him about Cambodia and Laos. His reply was that Vietminh's relations with the resistance movements in those countries
were on an international basis, and that the movement which

Ho Chi Minh headed was confined to Vietnam proper, i.e., Annam, Tonkin and the territories belonging to the old Empire.

When I returned his call, a few days later, I asked him about the prospects of a truce in Indo-China and of a settlement of the problem by negotiations. His answer was: "What is there to negotiate? The French have only to go away. We are prepared at all times to negotiate about that. But a truce without France accepting beforehand to evacuate our country would only mean giving a respite to the weary French forces." Hoang also told me that the French were very distrustful of Americans, and while prepared to accept financial and military assistance hated the idea of having American advisers attached to Bao Dai's Government. Bao Dai in his turn was playing the Americans against the French.

In June the political atmosphere began to clear a little. Dean Acheson's evidence before the Senate Committee declared positively that America was agreeable "to a reliable cease-fire on the 38th parallel," and that neither the U.S. nor the U.N. had any intention of bringing about the unity of Korea by military action. He expressed himself ready also to discuss the question of the admission of China to the United Nations. Immediately I wired to Delhi requesting the Ministry to ascertain officially from Washington whether the State Department desired this question to be taken up with the Chinese. But nothing very much came out of this, as the Americans were not yet prepared to make a formal proposal. Things, however, were definitely moving. On the 24th of June, the anniversary of the Korean war, Yakov Malik made his famous offer of a cease-fire at the 38th parallel and this took the world by surprise. Everyone seemed pleased. The Americans, the British, and the Chinese agreed that the time had come to discuss cease-fire. I advised Delhi to be cautious as in my opinion the Russian move was meant only to put the Americans in the wrong, or as Wezikopf explained to me, "to carry the struggle on to another plane." That in fact it was so was proved by the fact that it took over eighteen months of negotiations to reach the cease-fire agreement.

CHAPTER XI

A TOUR IN THE INTERIOR

I HAD been over a year in Peking but had not seen anything of the country outside Peking, Tientsin, and Shanghai. Early in spring I had planned to go to Manchuria but Mr. Nehru advised me in view of the Korean situation to remain at headquarters as no one knew how things might develop from day to day. When the truce negotiations started, however, the position seemed clear enough to enable me to undertake a tour and see things for myself in the interior. Accordingly I informed the Chinese Foreign Office of my desire to travel in the North Western Region and received the necessary permission without undue delay. The original plan was to go to Sian and Lanchow and from there through the Gobi desert to the famous Tunghuan Caves on the borders of Sinkiang. But my wife insisted on including Yenan also, though that town was out of the way and quite inaccessible by ordinary methods of communication. I tried to dissuade her but she mentioned the matter directly to Chou En-lai once when he came to dinner and he not only agreed to the suggestion but warmly welcomed it. A few days later we were told that everything had been arranged for the journey and a special aeroplane was being put at our disposal for our tour.

My party consisted of my wife and daughter and a Chinese-speaking secretary, Dr. Virendra Kumar. The Foreign Office sent with us a young English-speaking officer, Lang Shin-kang, to look after our convenience and to be a liaison officer with local authorities. We had been very friendly with Lang from the beginning of our stay in Peking and we were very glad to have him, especially as he was well aware of my wife's special requirements in the matter of food. At our request a photographer was also added to the party. We left on the 21st of August and reached Sian before lunch. We were received with great courtesy by the leading officials of the local Government. Arrangements had been made for us to stay in the house of General Yang, who under the orders of "the young marshal" Chang Huseh-liang had arrested and imprisoned Chiang Kai-shek in 1936, for which act of temerity he had later to pay not only with his life but with the complete rooting-out of his family to three generations.

Sian is an epitome of early Chinese history. Known then as Chang An, it was the capital of the two great indigenous dynasties of China, the Han and the Tang, and was in fact the most important city in the country till the Mongols founded Peking and made it their capital. Around it are many historical sites, such as the tomb of the first Emperor Chin Shih Huang Ti, the sulphur springs of Lin Tun Shan, where Yang Kwei Fei, considered the most beautiful woman of China, held her orgies which wellnigh brought down the Tangs, where later Chiang Kai-shek was arrested while engaged in planning his campaign against the communists, the great tower erected in honour of Hiuen Tsang, the celebrated pilgrim who returned from India loaded with relics and books. In Sian is also situated the academy of inscriptions, the earliest of its kind, which houses a unique collection of documents and books engraved on stone, one of the most interesting of which is the Sian-fu tablet which describes the arrival of the Christian priest Olopin in A.D. 635 "bearing the true sacred books."

Besides visiting the public institutions arranged by local authorities, I went without notice to many wayside villages to see for myself the effects of agrarian reforms and the changes brought about by the revolution. Curiosity also took me to Lin Tun Shan, the hillside resort of Yang Kwei Fei. It is now frequented by workers for whose benefit special buses are run from Sian. I was accompanied on my visit by an officer who had the privilege of guarding Chiang during his imprisonment. From him I heard the story of the arrest. What he told me was that when Yang surrounded the place with his soldiers and after overcoming the guards forced his entry into the pavilion, Chiang who was then resting in his underwear climbed the wall with the help of a nephew of his and jumped to the other side and fled into the jungle behind. We walked up to the place where he tried to hide.

There he was discovered by General Yang's men and taken in a jeep to Sian. Though the weather was bitterly cold, Chiang it would seem asked many times for water during the short drive of forty-five minutes. In Sian the Generalissimo was kept closely guarded. Chiang seems to have been totally overwhelmed by this unexpected turn of events and refused to take food, perhaps out of fear of being poisoned. The officer also added that till Chou En-lai arrived from Yenan, Chiang was afraid of being shot by his captors. On the walls of the pavilion someone has written a poem in Chinese to commemorate this incident. Freely translated its meaning is as follows:

> A great thieving animal was caught here
> but it was let off, when we discovered,
> that it was no wolf
> but a jackal.

Lin Tun Shan may well be described as the hill of the triple tragedy in Chinese history. The earliest story associated with it is that of an emperor who lost his throne in his effort to please a morose wife. The lady could not be made to smile and therefore the emperor in order to please her had the beacon lights lit on the Lin Tun Shan, which was the traditional signal for summoning the feudatories in case of danger to the capital. The feudatories arrived post haste in response to the signal but were told that it was all a mistake. Seeing their discomfiture, the empress was pleased to smile. But as luck would have it, a few months later the barbarians actually appeared before the capital. The beacons were again lit, but the feudatories thinking that it was another joke failed to arrive and the capital easily fell to the enemy. The second occasion was when Huang Ming, the "Brilliant Emperor," the most talented monarch of the Tang dynasty, became a puppet in the hands of Yang Kwei Fei. It was this lady who built palaces and pavilions around the sulphur springs. Her revelries in this place led to a rebellion which drove the emperor out of his capital and forced a discontented soldiery to hang her in front of the emperor. The third and most sensational incident was the arrest of the Generalissimo.

As there were many places connected with Hiuen Tsang around

K

Sian, I found it interesting to stay a few days more in Sian than I had originally intended. The Faith Propagating temple erected in Hiuen Tsang's honour which is situated about thirty miles away from Sian was specially interesting because the great pilgrim's tomb is in a shrine attached to it. The extensive buildings of the temple are now used as a school and in the guest house "young pioneers"—the communist equivalent of "boy scouts"—meet for their activities. But I was glad to notice some ash of recently-burnt incense.

In the villages we visited we saw ample evidence of revolutionary activity. Everyone had taken the "national pledge" and walls were as usual plastered with slogans of Resist America, Aid Korea. People were keenly interested in the land reform and I, through my own interpreter, discussed with some of the farmers their special problems. The villages I visited had also peasants' organizations, study groups, women's organizations, and the entire paraphernalia of New Democracy. The chairman of the Women's Association, a lady of old times, with lily foot, discoursed to me at length on the progressive character of the new marriage laws. I asked her how many marriages had been registered under the new law. Only two; how many divorces? One, was her reply. The marriage revolution had not evidently penetrated so far. The association is, however, active. The chairman told me with pride that her association had 126 members—practically the entire adult women population of the village—and that they were divided into six groups: production, hand spinning and weaving, study, culture, etc.

On the last day of our stay in Sian, the local Government invited us to a special dramatic and dance entertainment by the "culture group" of the city. The Minister of Culture was a democrat and a scholar in the old style, a great admirer of Tang poetry, who was ready to quote Li Po and Tu Fu at the slightest provocation. The entertainment he put on for us was very interesting, a combination of the old and the new as almost everything else is in China. It began with two scenes from a Shensi opera based on a story from the annals of *The Three Kingdoms*. Its theme was the jealousy that a victorious general felt towards the chief minister, on the plausible argument that but for his strategic abilities the State itself would have been destroyed and there would have been no place for a chief minister. His claim therefore was that the civil authorities should be considered inferior in rank and position to him. It is the queen that mediates in the quarrel and brings the presumptuous general to see the wisdom of allowing the affairs of the State to be run by civil authorities. Everything of course ends well, with the general visiting the chief minister and apologizing to him for his lack of understanding. The acting was in the traditional style with make-ups, masks and symbolic gestures similar to those in the Peking opera. This was followed by songs and dances with a strong political bias. A group of Mongolian boys and girls first put on a dance which was described as *New Life in Mongolia*, meant to depict the happiness and freedom in which they lived under the new regime. Another item, called *The Dawn in Sinkiang*, was by Kazak and Uighar boys and girls. It opened with a song, the first tune of which roughly translated meant "Oh Sinkiang, our beautiful Sinkiang, you are sunk under feudal oppression." This is sung in an atmosphere of gloom and darkness: then suddenly light begins to appear. It is the People's Liberation Army coming to Sinkiang, and joyous dance and music follow. It was of course political propaganda but propaganda done with beauty and artistry.

From Sian we flew to Yenan—the celebrated cave city which was Mao Tse-tung's headquarters for eleven years. It was only when we got into the plane that we were told that the airstrip in Yenan which had not been used for many years had to be specially repaired under Chairman Mao's orders to enable our plane to land there and that was the reason for the slight delay in arranging our programme. Yenan is about 200 miles from Sian. The intervening country is full of impassable ridges and canyons and almost uninhabited and one could well understand why Mao Tse-tung selected this place as his headquarters after the long march. The town is on the banks of a river which flows through a gorge, affording natural facilities for cave construction. On both sides of the river, a city with twenty thousand cave habitations, housing universities, hospitals, party headquarters, organs of the liberated area government, etc., had come into being during the days of Mao's occupation. Today it presents a deserted appearance, though every effort is being made by the Peking Government to maintain its importance.

Yenan had a niche in Chinese history even before the communists made it their headquarters. The great poet, Tu Fu, who shares with Li Po the throne of Chinese literature, took shelter there during the Turki rebellion in the time of Huang Ming, the Tang Emperor. It is in this place that he is reported to have composed some of his most brilliant anti-war poems which may be read in Waley's translations. There is also in Yenan a cave of 10,000 Buddhas, a Buddhist retreat ornamented by many images of Sakyamuni sculptured in rock. During the period of communist occupation this cave housed the *Liberation Daily*, a crudely-printed sheet whose articles, however, were scanned with care in Tokyo, no less than in Nanking, in London no less than in Washington, as it was the mouthpiece of Mao Tse-tung and the People's Liberation Army.

We stayed two days in Yenan visiting the historic sites, the caves where Mao Tse-tung, Chou En-lai, and others used to live, the building where the famous session of the communist party was held which decided on a coalition government, the plot where Mao cultivated tobacco for his own and his friends' use, the Yang family garden where Chu Teh, an inveterate tree planter and gardener, had planted peach trees, the valley of culture where was situated the Lu Hsun college of art, the site of the anti-Japanese war academy where Lin Piao trained his cadres, the hospital in which the Indian medical mission worked, etc. From the Yang family garden, I arranged for some peaches to be sent to Chu Teh, as I was told those were the trees he himself had planted and that he had never been back there since the trees began to bear fruit.

Yenan is unimportant as a town now; but a visit to it is important as without it no one can understand fully what is happening in China. It was the laboratory in which the political and economic experiments of new China were tried out on a large scale. It is the "blockade economy" which the communists developed in Yenan that gives them the confidence in their struggle against the embargo which the U.S.A. is enforcing against China. It is the austerity that the leaders and the cadres developed in these barren regions, where they had to make the soil yield the utmost, develop an industry out of primitive conditions, create by human labour what everywhere is done with the help of machines, that provides the basic experience, strength, and discipline of the present Chinese Government.

My most interesting experience in Yenan was a visit I paid to a mountain village just outside the town. In this area land revolution had taken place in 1935, before even Mao Tse-tung reached there. The leader of the movement there was Kao Kang, the present chairman of the People's Government of the North-East (Manchuria). As the village land had been distributed over fifteen years ago, I thought it would be worth while to see how things had developed. The village is situated about 500 feet above the road leading outside Yenan. People live in caves bored in the hill-side, and cultivation as on the lower ranges of the Himalayas is in terraced plots. Cotton, castor oil, wheat, and millet are grown. There are only eleven families in the village. The chairman of the village came to Yenan as a wandering beggar in 1938 and was allotted the usual seven mows of land (an acre and a quarter) for himself and his wife. There he evolved "a mutual aid" system by which he shared the implements and animals of his neighbours for giving some of his wife's and his labour to a neighbouring family. He prospered and when K.M.T. re-occupied Yenan in 1947 he left with the communists and came back again in 1948. He was given back his land but this time there were no implements or animals for himself or his neighbours. Then six out of the eleven families joined under his leadership in a mutual aid team, with shares worked out on the basis of adult labour power. Thus he with his two nephews and nieces-in-law contribute five units to the labour pool: others in the same way. They cultivate the fields jointly and share out the produce. Implements, manure, etc., are bought in common, each family contributing according to the area it owns. I talked not only to him but to some others of the "team" and found that the system had worked remarkably well, increasing production, providing suitable implements and manure, and better means of sale. For his success in this "mutual aid team" system the old man has been elected Labour Hero of the country.

"The mutual aid team in cultivation" is a very important step and is nationally encouraged both as solving the problem of fragmentized land, and secondly as a step to collectivization. It is in fact a collectivization in miniature proceeding from the people and not imposed by the State. It seemed to me much more effective than the complicated system of land consolidation attempted in different parts of India. It provided education in rural leadership, mutual help, and an elementary co-operative system. The difficulty in India would be the tendency to take the disputes arising out of labour-shares to courts. Here it is not permitted. The village council decides the dispute.

We spent a considerable time with the family of the labourer in his cave and were treated to bean soup and tea and parted in great friendliness. The cave had the usual mud-built bed, a number of large china jars to keep dried vegetables, a wooden store for grain, and a stove for winter. The adjacent cave connected by a door in the "wall" was used as kitchen, etc. The caves were decorated (as everywhere else) with pictures of national heroes, a copy of the national pact which all adult members of the family had signed, to increase production, to protect the property of the nation, to resist America, aid Korea, etc. Seeing the farmer and his prosperous family discussing the budget of next year and his hopes of increased production, it was almost impossible to believe that he and his wife had been wandering beggars only thirteen years ago.

From Yenan we returned to Sian, and left the next day for Lanchow. Though it is one of the most famous places in China for natural beauty, we did not stop there on our outward journey as the Sino-Soviet planes fly only twice a week. So we went on to Chiao Chuan, an oasis in the Gobi desert situated about 350 miles to the west of Lanchow. The country to the west of Lanchow for a distance of about a hundred miles is covered with high mountain ranges with snow-clad peaks. This range forms the natural boundary of China proper. The desert officially begins on the other side of the range, called in Chinese the seven ranged mountains, though it was clear from the air that the desert has been encroaching rapidly. Till quite recent times the area between the mountains and Chiao Chuan must have been a fertile plain for many river beds and large oases can still be seen. But the movement of the desert has been irresistible.

Chiao Chuan is the seat of a Commissioner's government. It is a pleasant and extensive oasis and forms an important centre of supply and communication to Sinkiang. A 650-mile motor road which connects Lanchow with Ansi, another large oasis in the desert, passes through Chiao Chuan. From here our journey was by weapon carriers, jeeps, and trucks which had been provided by the local authorities, who also gave us an escort of thirty men of the P.L.A. We had to carry everything with us, beds, blankets, provisions, cooks, and servants.

The desert was said to be infested with gangs of bandits who operate from inaccessible mountains which in some parts come quite near to the road. The Chinese Government had therefore ordered that special precautionary measures should be taken for the safety of the party and when our convoy stopped anywhere even for a minute the army personnel immediately rushed to the most advantageous posts with their machine-guns.

Compared to the Gobi, the Indian desert, in the middle of which I had lived for nine years, is a very tame affair. The Indian desert is of soft sand, with quite a lot of shrubbery and a great deal of natural life—birds, for example. The Gobi on the other hand is not sandy. It is hard and crusted and for thirty and forty miles at a stretch there is no sign of any kind of life. One sees but rarely birds, or other living things. Also there is no vegetation, merely a vast expanse of dark, hardened soil, where even camels do not tread during day. Leaving Chiao Chuan, our first halt was at a place a hundred miles farther to the west, known as Yu Men, or the Jade Gate. It is now an oasis of respectable size, not less than thirty or forty square miles. At one time the Great Wall of China extended to this place. It was its farthest extension to the west. At that time, as the name the Jade Gate suggests, it must have been the limit of the Gobi desert. But during the last few hundred years the desert has encroached much into the interior, leaving Yu Men an oasis.

One thing I noticed here apart from the usual construction

work—carried on as elsewhere without interruption—was that army units were engaged in extensive agricultural operations, probably for the supply of forces scattered over the area. By evening time we reached An Si (which means Western Peace), a small town another hundred miles inside the desert. Here the local government had reserved a roadside inn named "Three Friends" entirely for our use. Though it was no more than a mud hut with a few rooms, the local authorities had put in carpets, beds, etc., and converted it into a suitable place for a night's rest.

A road from An Si goes to the Tunghuang village from where the caves lie at a distance of two miles. There is only a rough track to the side of the mountain and up to the very last minute no opening could be seen anywhere, no evidence of human occupation or of any activity. When we reached the hill, there was a gap like a side entrance from which a river must have once emerged, for it was clearly a river bed. Once you enter the gap, the sight that greets you is something for which you have not been prepared. You see before you a small valley, apparently surrounded on all sides by hills, a garden enclosed by nature. It has two gaps both invisible from outside unless one comes very near to the site: one through which the river, now dry, entered the valley, and the other through which it emerged into the desert to disappear in the parched sands. One side of the valley is green with recently-planted poplars and a tiny rivulet runs by it. Behind the poplars lie the range where Buddhist monks over 1,400 years ago built their caves for retirement and meditation and embellished them with paintings, which are amongst the supreme expressions of mural art, comparable only to the cave paintings of Ajanta, Bagh, and Sigiri.

The authorities had arranged for us to be put up in a newly-constructed building meant to serve as a local museum. It is a modern type of building with a pleasant garden attached to it. Facing the building are the caves and on both sides the officers of the Tunghuang Institute have planted ornamental and useful trees and vegetable gardens. Sweet melons, perhaps the sweetest in the world, native to Sinkiang, have been brought and cultivated successfully, the local officials even claiming that they taste better than their Sinkiang originals. They are undoubtedly as delicious as the best Lucknow *Kharbujas*. Though it was only the first of September the weather was exceptionally fine, bright, and sunny but cool during day and quite cold at night. The air was bracing and as in all desert areas the night was particularly fresh with a clear and star-studded sky. Altogether it seemed an ideal place at this time of the year. But the institute officials warned me that the winter in Tunghuang was extremely severe, with the temperature generally several degrees below zero. This severe winter extends for over five months. It is difficult to imagine how the monks lived and worked there in the winter months, but it seems certain that they lived in the caves all the year round.

The "discovery" of Tunghuang and the suddenness with which it leapt into world fame constitute one of the romances of twentieth-century exploration and archaeology. Tunghuang had of course never been forgotten in China, though the caves were uncared for and the general public had neglected them. Even stray foreigners had visited the caves in the nineteenth century. Count Szechenyi's expedition visited Tunghuang in 1867 and one of its members, Professor L. de Loczy, has left a glowing description of the paintings in the caves. But neither the Chinese public generally, nor the world at large, knew anything about the existence of Tunghuang until Sir Aurel Stein announced to the world the discovery of the great library hidden away and walled up in one of the caves.

Prof. Loczy's descriptions of Tunghuang had fired Stein's imagination and after exploring many parts of Sinkiang and the ruins of cities in the Gobi desert, following the footsteps of Hiuen Tsang he arrived at last in Tunghuang with a party of Indian assistants and a Chinese secretary. In the desert he had heard through a man named Zahid Beg, "vague rumours about a great hidden deposit of ancient manuscripts which was said to have been discovered accidentally in one of the grottoes." It was said that these manuscripts were not in Chinese and under orders from Peking they had been locked up again. Stein's desire was to get hold of these. The manuscript hoard was under the care of a Taoist priest named Wang Tao-shih, who was totally ignorant of their value. He was a kind of self-appointed guardian of the grottoes and with money collected through his personal effort had built a nine storeyed temple in one of the grottoes to cover the immense statue of the Buddha which attracted his innocent mind because of its size. How Stein by persuasion, duplicity and by a little money overcame the scruples of Wang can best be described in his own words:

"The presence of this quaint priest, with his curious mixture of pious zeal, naïve ignorance, and astute tenacity of purpose forcibly called to my mind those early Buddhist pilgrims who, simple in mind but strong in faith and superstition, once made their way to India in the face of formidable difficulties.

"More than once before, my well-known attachment to the memory of Hiuen Tsang, the greatest of those pilgrims, had been helpful in securing me a sympathetic hearing both among the learned and the simple. Wang Tao-shih, too, had probably heard about it. So, surrounded by these tokens of lingering Buddhist worship, genuine though distorted, I thought it appropriate to tell Wang Tao-shih, as well as my poor Chinese would permit, of my devotion to the saintly traveller; how I had followed his footsteps from India for over 10,000 li across inhospitable mountains and deserts; how in the course of this pilgrimage I had traced to its present ruins, however inaccessible, many a sanctuary he had piously visited and described; and so on."

This argument seems to have had some effect on Wang who allowed Stein's secretary to carry to his tent a bundle of rolls. The very first examination showed that the bundles contained "sutras from Buddhist canons which the colophons declared to have been brought from India and translated by Hiuen Tsang himself." Stein felt justified in calling upon the saint again and had it hinted to Wang that it was the intervention of the spirit of Hiuen Tsang that led to so unexpected a discovery and the saint would only be pleased if the books were presented to Stein, of course for a consideration. "Under the influence of that quasi-divine hint," says Stein, "he now summoned courage to open before me the rough door closing the narrow entrance which led from the side of the broad front passage into the rock-caved recess, at a level of about four feet above the floor of the former. The sight of the small room disclosed was one to make my eyes open wide. Heaped up in layers, but without any order, there appeared in the dim light of the priest's lamp a solid mass of manuscript bundles rising to a height of nearly ten feet, and filling, as subsequent measurement showed, close on five hundred cubic feet."

When some of these bundles were examined they were found to contain not only manuscripts in many languages, but also paintings of exceptional beauty on fine gauze-like silk and linen, representing Bodhisattvas and scenes from Buddhist legend. The question of acquiring this had become urgent. Says Stein: "Then, tired as we all were, I took the occasion to engage the priest in another long talk about our common hero and patron saint, the great Hiuen Tsang. What better proof of his guidance and favour could I claim than that I should have been allowed to behold such a wonderful hidden store of sacred relics belonging to his own times and partly derived, perhaps, from his Indian wanderings, within a cave-temple which so ardent an admirer of 'T'ang-seng' had restored and was now guarding? Again I let the Tao-shih enlarge, as we stood in the loggia, upon the extraordinary adventures of his great saint as depicted in those cherished frescoes on its walls. The panel which showed Hiuen Tsang returning with his animal heavily laden with sacred manuscripts from India, was the most effective apologue I could advance for my eager interest in the relics the Tao-shih had discovered and was yet keeping from daylight.

"The priest in his more susceptible moods could not help acknowledging that this fate of continued confinement in a dark hole was not the purpose for which the great scholar-saint had let him light upon these precious remains of Buddhist lore, and that he himself was quite incompetent to do justice to them by study or otherwise. Was it not evident, so Chiang (Stein's Chinese secretary) pleaded with all the force of his soft reasoning, that by allowing me, a faithful disciple of Hiuen Tsang, to render accessible to western students the literary and other relics which a providential discovery had placed so abundantly in his keeping, he would do an act of real religious merit? That this pious concession would also be rewarded by an ample donation for the benefit of the shrine he had laboured to restore to its old glory, was a secondary consideration merely to be hinted at."

With this argument to help him Stein acquired and brought away from Tunghuang 9,000 manuscripts and paintings for a paltry sum of 500 rupees. When the news of Stein's discovery with its rare Sanskrit texts so long considered lost and precious paintings came to be known, it created a great sensation in the world of scholarship. The very next year the great French scholar, Pelliot, emulated Stein and did the job even more thoroughly. He ransacked the library so systematically that when Stein visited the caves a few years later no manuscript of value was left there for anyone to acquire.

When the acquisition and transfer to Western capitals of this great collection of books came to be known, it not only aroused public indignation in China, but created widespread interest in academic and scholarly circles about the caves themselves. The Kuomintang Government also took steps to establish an Institute at Tunghuang under competent artists. The authorities of New China were quick to realize the immense value of this great repository of ancient Chinese art and have now taken it under their special care. A great exhibition was held in Peking in the spring of 1951 in the Forbidden City, where copies in colour of representative work from most of the caves executed by modern Chinese artists were made available to the general public. Thus the wheel has come round again and after the neglect of seven centuries, Tunghuang is becoming once more the centre of a great artistic revival.

The lower half of the mountain-side facing the valley seems to have been plastered and painted when Tunghuang was in its full glory. Only here and there some of the painting has survived the neglect of centuries. In some places stray *Apsara* figures of Indian mythology could be seen painted on the mountain itself, whose proportions clearly testify to their being part of a larger design. Inside in the 460 caves beginning with the time of the Wei dynasty (sixth century) and ending with the Yuans (thirteenth century), covering a period of 700 years, there can be found an immense artistic effort, a veritable treasure house of painting, decoration and design. The idea of the rock-cut temple itself is derived from India. Apart from this, and the figures and legends of Buddhism which form the subject-matter of the art of Tunghuang, many of the striking features of these caves are borrowed from India. Thus, as Silcock has observed, "the painted ceilings are divided into rectangular panels in the semblance of the real coffers and beams of Indian architecture." The circular and three-sided arches, covering the niches carved from the rock, are also of Indian origin. The *pipal* leaf motif, also a common feature, comes directly from India and of course is connected with the sacredness of the *bodhi* tree. These features continued to the end, even after the paintings in Tunghuang had become predominantly Chinese. The earliest-dated cave was painted in A.D. 572 in the time of the Wei emperors. Tunghuang is therefore at least 200 years later than the earlier caves of Ajanta and contemporaneous with some of its later caves. The best work in painting as well as design was done in the earlier caves, though the paintings of the Tang period also are marked by perfection of technique and a genuineness of inspiration. But the Tang painting had already become a little luxurious and decadent, at least so far as Buddhist painting was concerned. While the Wei painting was vigorous, and composition perfect in every way, the Tang art tended to become elegant and formalistic with over-decoration of figure and ornaments and stylization of form. Also the Wei period painting shows greater influence of Indian art. More especially in some of the famous Jataka story panels, depicting the incidents from the Buddha's earlier births, such as the Bodhisattva giving the eagle a piece of his own flesh in exchange for the life of a dove, or the prince who sacrificed himself in order that the starving tigress and her cubs might live, both painted in the Wei period, the Indian inspiration and technique are clearly marked.

Though the Wei period was thus the most constructive, the Tang caves cannot be considered merely as imitative or decadent. The artistic genius of the Chinese achieved its most characteristic expression in poetry, painting, and sculpture during this period of national greatness. During the early and middle Tang periods, the Wei inspiration is continued, but there is a change in colouring, technique and treatment, the Tang painters using a kind of chemical dye which has become discoloured with time. The panels are much larger, with numerous personages crowding the scene and a new type of human figure is evolved, which combines Indian and Chinese characteristics. The stories are no longer the simple tales of Buddha's sacrifices, but those relating to Buddhist controversies with the Brahmins. A popular theme is the gift by a prince of the royal umbrella to the Buddha which the king, under the influence of the Brahmins, attempted to recover. On this, the prince, his wife and children and their attendants become monks. This story is painted in different variations in many caves. Another favourite theme with the Tang artists in the larger caves is the representation of the Pure Land of the West (India). After the return of the early pilgrims and especially of Hiuen Tsang, India seems to have captured Chinese imagination as the Holy Land of Pure Virtue and the Tang artists gave free play to their imagination in depicting scenes from the holy land. In three very large caves may be seen colossal images of the Buddha after his *parinirvana*, with his disciples lamenting the loss of the master. Here the Tang artists excelled themselves, for the statues are remarkable for their grace, proportion and delicacy. The walls of the caves depict scenes of the familiar story of the kings of the countries where the Buddha had lived and preached arriving to mourn and to claim a share of his remains. The Tang artists are also responsible for two other immense images of the Buddha in a sitting posture, one of which is over sixty metres in height. The paintings on the walls of this cave were unfortunately destroyed by the Taoist priest who, however, erected a nine-storeyed pagoda to cover the statue. The smaller image, twenty metres in height, equally beautiful, may be seen in the cave as the Tang artists left it. The walls of this immense cave are covered with paintings of rare beauty. Altogether it may be said that the Tang caves, though they are more sophisticated than the Wei and Sui caves, and show less genuine devotion, still contain masterpieces of the painter's and sculptor's arts.

In the later Tang caves (A.D. 800–900) there is a marked falling off. The fleshy cheeks and obviously contented and self-satisfied expression of the later Tang figures in these caves reflect little of the serenity and spiritual calm of Buddhism. The love of all created beings, the poise and happiness given by faith, the very austerity of life—all of which are essential aspects of great Buddhist art, including the art of the Wei period in Tunghuang—seem to become less and less marked as centuries rolled on.

In the period of the five dynasties (907–960) when the Tunghuang area passed under the great Turki family of Tsao some fine work was again done. A Tsao ruler opened two large caves which were decorated with beautiful painting dealing with the Buddha's life. With the Sungs (1000–1200) a new tradition starts. The artists not only opened new caves, installing large images of the Buddha and painting numerous murals, but they also painted new layers on earlier panels. In some places the two layers are plainly visible. There is noticeable decay in taste and the paintings are not of the same quality as those of the Wei or Tang periods.

The contribution of the Mongol dynasty was the introduction of *tantrism* which seems particularly incongruous in the atmosphere of Tunghuang. The *tantric* gods and goddesses of Lamaism, a variation of the Indian *Sakti* cult with their *maithuna* pictures make their appearance in these later caves. From the artistic point of view they are not without force or beauty.

Though the predominant motive of the paintings in the Tunghuang caves is Buddhist, it should not be thought that all the pictures are religious or deal with the life of the Buddha. In numerous caves there can be seen pictures of the daily lives of the common people, men and women engaged in normal occupations, ploughing, harvesting, milking, governors going in procession, ladies being carried in sedan chairs, etc. Pictures representing dancing, music and general enjoyment are also not uncommon. One interesting panel represents people of various provinces in China going on pilgrimage to a holy mountain in Shansi.

The creative effort in these caves continued for over 600 years, with varying degrees of inspiration. They form indeed a veritable treasure house for Asia as a whole, for the caves were inhabited, at least during the first three centuries, by a great international community of monks. Though the work was done predominantly

by the Chinese artists as the decorations and some of the characteristic early Chinese motives clearly prove, and the religious inspiration and perhaps the early techniques came from India, there is
evidence of Persian, Turkish, and other influences at work. A great
international religion like Buddhism recognized no differences of
race and nationality and the innumerable monastic cells must have
housed thousands of pious monks from all parts of Asia.

From the point of view of Chinese history Tunghuang is of very
special importance as it provides an unsurpassed record of life
through many centuries: pictures of costumes at different periods,
modes of transport, architectural designs, etc.

There is reason to think that Tunghuang has not yielded all her
secrets to the world. Recent discoveries indicate that there is at
least another set of about a hundred caves buried in sand, which may
prove to have been even better preserved than those now opened.
The Tunghuang Institute is studying plans now for exploring these
caves.

It is impossible to conclude the description of this visit without
alluding to one of the most extraordinary cases of vandalism
perpetrated in the name of scholarship. We in India are familiar
with the theft of artistic treasure. Tunghuang also suffered from
such activities by acquisitive scholars: but the amazing attempt of
an American named Warner, who tried by a chemical process to
transfer the mural paintings themselves to specially prepared
cloth and take them away to America, thereby spoiling some of
the most beautiful panels beyond repair, is without parallel in the
theft of artistic treasures. He is reported to have carried away
twenty-four such pictures, but a second and more comprehensive
attempt was fortunately foiled by the just anger of the Chinese
public.

In regard to the future work at Tunghuang one thing seemed to
be a clear necessity. It is of vital importance to the work both in
India and in China that those responsible for the preservation of
cave paintings should co-operate closely. It is necessary that the
work in Ajanta and Bagh should be studied carefully in the light of
Tunghuang and *vice versa*. The visit of Dr. Dchang, the Director of
the Tunghuang Institute, as a member of the Cultural Mission to

India a few months later, was perhaps the first step in this direction.

We may conclude this brief survey of the immortal caves of Tunghuang with a few observations. How did so large a monastery, with a vigorous artistic and cultural life, come to exist in the middle of the Gobi desert? Was it sheer perversity, a desire to lead a life of contemplation away from the madding crowd, that led the monks to establish themselves in this walled-up, tiny oasis? How is it that after over 700 years of unceasing activity, the caves with their artistic treasures and the great library were abandoned by their occupants? These questions cannot yet be decisively answered, but the discoveries of archaeologists and historians make it possible for us to understand something of the causes that led to the growth, decay and abandonment of Tunghuang.

As is well known, by the fifth century A.D., Buddhism had established itself firmly in China. The intervening territory between China proper which then extended to An Si (eighty miles from Tunghuang) and the Indian borders would seem to have been under local rulers who were staunchly Buddhist. Kumarajiva, the first great missionary who came to China, the son of a Kuchean princess and an Indian father, himself belonged to one of these kingdoms. At least from his time a great and continuous traffic developed between India and China along this route. Sir Aurel Stein's explorations have unearthed many monasteries and cave temples right from the Indian frontier to Tunghuang. In the cave temples of Sinkiang, the paintings are, I am informed, of even superior excellence to those of Tunghuang. It is therefore fair to presume that these cave temples and monasteries were established as rest houses and *dharma salas* for pilgrims and missionaries on their way to and from India. The Tunghuang caves represented the last stage of the long journey from India, as the Great Wall of China extended at that time to An Si (Western Peace). Also, Tunghuang was on the main line of communications with the Byzantine and Arab West, with which areas also, under the Tang emperors, economic and commercial relations had developed to some extent.

With the tenth century, when communications with India became infrequent as a result of both the decay of Buddhism in

L

India and the penetration of Islam into the Kabul valley, Tunghuang and the other cave temples on this route began to decay. For
a time the area passed under Tibetan control which explains the
prevalence of *tantric* motives in some of the later caves. Finally
with the upheavals in Central Asia, following Mongol conquest,
the vigorous cultural life of that area of which Tunghuang was an
expression was practically destroyed. Before abandoning the
caves, the monks seem to have taken the precaution of concealing
the great collection of books which they were unable to carry
away. There they remained under the protecting cover of sand
till the Taoist Wang in his well-meant effort to restore one of the
caves discovered them and stood guard on it, like the fabled Jinn
over a treasure, without knowing what it contained and how
valuable it was.

Today there is a new life of intense activity in Tunghuang, not
indeed of opening new caves and decorating them with paintings
depicting scenes from the Buddha's life, but of steady research,
preservation and copying. The desert is being made to yield its
secrets and with the establishment of a school of arts and a
museum at the caves, a revival of Sino-Indian artistic traditions
may be witnessed in these desert areas where the two countries
co-operated so fruitfully many centuries ago.

We returned to Lanchow by a special plane which was kindly
sent to bring us. In Lanchow I visited a village where land reform
had been given effect to only partially, the special college for
national minorities, and the workers' palace of culture.

The village which I visited is situated in one of the eighteen
islands in the Hoang Ho (the yellow river) and could only be
reached by a sheepskin raft. The yellow river at Lanchow is so
rapid and treacherous that no boats ply on it. The raft which is
used is made by tying together into a square a number of inflated
sheepskins. It cannot be used to go against the current and is
therefore allowed to float down the river. It appeared safe enough
once we were on it, but the experience of going down on a small
raft in one of the most dangerous currents was certainly exciting.
We reached the island after about half an hour of this journey.

The village Yenthen consists of 71 houses and has a

population of 200. The soil is perhaps one of the most fertile in the world, being formed from the loess brought down by the river. It was formed only about 200 years ago. We saw some such islands in the process of formation. There are seven villages in the island and we were received by Mr. Wei, who may be described as the headman of villages. The chairman of the village council, "a model peasant" named Li Han-fu and the more prominent peasants accompanied us. Land has not yet been distributed in the village. It was proposed to do so after the autumn harvest, i.e. in about another two months. But rents had been reduced by twenty-five per cent as from the date of the liberation and all illegal payments had been abolished. Li Han-fu himself is the owner of five mows (about an acre). Landlords, rich peasants, middle peasants, and poor peasants exist in the village. After liberation, the Government gave them seeds, fertilizers and implements and also helped them with money. Production has therefore been increased by over thirty per cent. A labour exchange system was in operation of which Mr. Li Han-fu was the leader. Forty-six people were enrolled in this team under which each one undertook to help others in their field work in his spare time. This increased available labour power for each field. Li Han-fu had been elected model peasant for the entire province of Kansu, he explained to me, on three grounds. First his general production record, secondly his leadership of the labour exchange system, thirdly for his general efficiency. He was wearing three medals and possessed a fourth one. Politically the village seemed highly educated, perhaps due to its proximity to the town. I asked them a number of questions about the "Aid Korea" movement and the villagers had all the answers at their fingers' ends. Undoubtedly the elimination of the landlord's exactions and the assistance given by the Government had created a new spirit in the village.

The College for National Minorities in Lanchow is one of the three institutions established by the Central People's Government in 1950: one in Peking as a central national institution, the second at Lanchow for the minorities of the north-west, and a third one at Chengtu for the tribes and minorities of the south-west. It is said that there are twenty-two national minority groups in the north-west. Actually there are only three, the Muslims, the Mongols, and the Tibetans, but the Chinese Government have split up the Muslims into many smaller racial units. Muslims technically mean only Chinese Muslims of Shensi and Kansu. The Muslims of Sinkiang are classed as Uighars, Kazaks, etc.

The Lanchow Minorities College is the central institution for the north-west. There are three other colleges, one at Chinghai mainly for Tibetans, a college in Sinkiang to serve local needs and another for Mongols. There are also mobile schools for giving short-term courses to minority groups.

At Lanchow, the Governor, a cousin of Ma Huang-kwei—the celebrated Muslim war lord—entertained us to a banquet. A few of the guests were Muslims like the Governor himself but they were Chinese—or Hans—and there was nothing to differentiate them from the rest. The banquet was specially notable for one dish—of python—which had been specially procured from Szechuan. During my stay in China I, like others, had been treated to many specialities which seem strange to people from other countries; but this was the first time that the flesh of python had been offered to me as a rare delicacy. At first I did not know what it was, but my daughter who understood some Chinese was able to make out from the conversation of our Chinese friends that it was the meat of a snake. On this I asked the Governor what it was, adding of course how delicious it tasted. The Governor was very pleased that I had expressed my appreciation of the dish, for he said it was python which could only be had in Szechuan. It tasted like the white meat of chicken, and whatever disinclination I might have felt to the taste of snake's flesh I was careful not to show, and to eat it as if I considered it something which I had long been waiting for.

The next day we returned by ordinary air service to Peking.

CHAPTER XII

THE END OF A MISSION

I HAD requested the Prime Minister to be posted to Egypt as a result of the advice of the doctors that my wife's restoration to normal health would require a prolonged stay in some warm and sunny country. I received permission to relinquish my post before winter and to return to India by October, but soon afterwards Mr. Nehru modified his orders and suggested that I should go back to China in February or March for a few more months so that I could bring to a conclusion one or two important questions which were under discussion and also help if possible in the final stages of the cease-fire negotiations in Korea. I therefore returned to India early in October. Instead of spending the winter months in India I requested that I might be allowed to go to Europe for the time in order to renew contacts and gain a first-hand appreciation of political developments in the West. As the General Assembly of the U.N. was meeting in Paris that year, Mr. Nehru suggested that I should join the delegation as it would enable me to meet the leaders of public opinion without causing undue speculation. But it was understood that I would be free to visit England and spend a part of the time there.

I arrived in Paris a few days after the Assembly session had been formally opened. B. N. Rau who was the leader of the delegation had already nominated me to the special political committee. As it was fully appreciated that I might not be able to devote much time to the important issues that came up before that body the Delegation also allotted to the Committee Mr. R. K. Nehru as my alternate and P. N. Haksar, chief of the political department of the High Commissioner's office, as adviser. The first question before the committee was the election of the chairman. Kaze Suchy, the Polish Permanent Representative, who had been advised of my presence in Paris by Burgin, approached me on the very first day with the suggestion that I should permit my name to be put forward for the chairmanship of the committee, in opposition to that of the Turkish delegate who was being supported by America and the N.A.T.O. powers. B. N. Rau was very pleased about it but it was difficult for me to accept the responsibilities of chairmanship in view of the programme I had in mind. Also I realized the political implications of the suggestion. So I excused myself, explaining frankly that I did not expect to stay in Paris for more than three or four weeks.

There was another curious incident during my stay in Paris which caused me much amusement. Naturally enough there was a great deal of public interest about conditions in China and I was always being pestered by correspondents for interviews and statements about the regime there. Some speeches of mine in Delhi had also caused considerable stir, especially in America. So I had utilized the opportunities that presented themselves to me to explain India's attitude towards the developments in the Far East, especially our relations with China. The Kuomintang representatives did not like this and they held a special press conference at which one of their leading delegates pronounced a violent tirade against me, accusing me of being a communist. It was significant that none of the papers took the least notice of what was said at that conference.

Though my stay in Paris was short, I met many of the political leaders of France and some of their leading newspaper commentators. The Quai d'Orsay, I noticed, was extremely well informed about conditions in China and had no ideological prejudices and confessed frankly that it was difficult for France to follow an independent policy in regard to China in view of the situation in Vietnam. All their enquiries turned finally to the single point: What do you think are the prospects of a negotiated agreement with Ho Chi Minh? I did my best to explain the Vietminh position as I knew it not only from Ambassador Hoang but also from other sources in Peking. From the letters which I have since received from French political personalities it would appear that my conversations had some effect—though it did not show itself at the time.

After three weeks in Paris, I crossed over to London where Krishna Menon had with characteristic thoroughness arranged a full and most useful programme for me. I met most people of importance in the Foreign Office—Eden, Selwyn Lloyd, Strang, Lord Reading and others. Lord Ismay, the Commonwealth Secretary, I had already known in India. Walter Monckton and I had worked together for many years in connection with the affairs of the princes of India. I had also some acquaintance with R. A. Butler. Krishna Menon insisted on treating my visit as being on duty and fixed up for me to see all the leading political figures in both parties, with whom I had most interesting conversations. The Prime Minister had written to Lord Mountbatten about my visit and he invited me privately to dine with him and Lady Mountbatten. The conversation was mainly about Kashmir, how the question should be handled in the Security Council as Graham's report was then under discussion. I found them both genuinely interested in the welfare of India and her good name. Lady Mountbatten seemed to be exceptionally well informed about what was happening everywhere in India and her frequent visits to the country had given her an insight into affairs which few people possessed. I considered it extremely fortunate that India should have two such good friends.

I had always admired Krishna Menon for his single-mindedness, for his clear vision of political objectives, and his unflagging zeal in the pursuit of those objectives. I knew of course that he had his detractors, especially among the entrenched civil services of India. I also knew that his notorious "incapacity to suffer fools gladly" made him numerous enemies. But I had no idea of the variety of his activities as High Commissioner. He ran students' hostels, clubs, and numerous other institutions for the welfare of the Indian community in London. He had also kept up his connection with the India League, an organization of British political leaders which he had founded during his career as an active politician in England. I noticed also that apart from his normal diplomatic activities, his permanent interest was in the younger generation, the large body of young men and women from India who came to England for higher studies. His relations with them were friendly and informal, and during the short period that I was in England with him, I must have accompanied him at least a dozen times to one institution or another where the High Commissioner mixed freely with the students and almost felt like one of them.

I returned to India by the end of the year. The six weeks I had in Europe had convinced me of two things. One was that the European nations, immersed in their own political and economic worries, would not be able materially to influence American action in the Far East; and consequently the tension in the Far East would not lessen and would continue till America decided on her own to try some alternative policy. The other was that France while anxious to bring to a conclusion the "Dirty War" in Indo-China would not be permitted to do so by the Americans: and, as a necessary corollary of this, the social and economic crisis in France would deepen as time went on. Secondly I was fortified in my conviction that for India to follow any other policy than the one which she was following—that of non-involvement in the cold war—would be suicidal, because the course of the cold war, whatever its origins, was being determined by the opportunist policies of the U.S. which did not take into consideration the interests of her allies, as was clear to me from her pressure on France to continue the war in Indo-China.

On arrival in India Pandit Nehru told me that he would like me to return at once to China and make one last effort to see whether we could not help to bring the Korean negotiations to a satisfactory conclusion. He was also desirous that I should see Thakin Nu, the Burmese Prime Minister, in Rangoon before leaving for Peking. During Thakin Nu's visit to Delhi in November he had discussed Sino-Burmese relations with me privately and when he left for Burma he had suggested to Mr. Nehru that I should be sent there for two or three days to meet the members of his Cabinet and discuss matters with them.

My visit to Burma was extremely useful. The Burmese Prime Minister, a man of saintly character who spends a great deal of his time in prayer and fasting, received me most cordially. He arranged for me to dine with the members of his Cabinet and we discussed in some detail the relations of Burma with China. There were two main questions which caused the Burmese Government deep concern; the first was of course the presence in Burma of the Kuomintang guerrillas and the fear that the communist forces in Yunnan might pursue these bandits across the border. The other was the question of the undefined boundary between Burma and China. I had more than once discussed the first point with the Chinese authorities at the instance of Mr. Nehru. At all discussions, I had been solemnly assured by Chou En-lai that so long as the Burmese Government continued to take adequate steps against the Kuomintang intruders, Peking would make no move which might create trouble for Burma. The second point I had never raised, as I had not been previously asked to do so. What the Burmese Government wanted to hear from me was a general appreciation of the situation in China in relation to South-East Asia, and more specifically whether in my judgment the Chinese would raise the question of the undefined boundary as the Kuomintang by various irregular acts had tried to do before its expulsion. The first question I discussed frankly, while in regard to the second I said that I was prepared to discuss matters informally with the Chinese Government if our Prime Minister authorized me to take it up.

The next day the Foreign Minister gave me a dinner which went on late into the night. The Burmese are a friendly people, always happy, with an infectious sense of humour. Though my plan was to take off in the early hours of the morning and I badly wanted some rest, they would not let me off, and kept on talking and telling amusing stories till two o'clock. Their excuse was that till about 11.30, the Chinese Ambassador had also been present at the dinner and that in his presence they had to be formal and well behaved and therefore they claimed that the party had begun only after his departure. Anyway the change in the atmosphere was very noticeable. I had the feeling that the Burmese generally were nervous of Chinese developments and felt not a little uneasy about the growth of a leviathan communist State just across their borders—a feeling which is, generally speaking, absent in India.

Since I visited Burma eighteen months before, things had improved beyond recognition. U Nu's personality had practically mastered the troubles, which had then seemed overwhelming. The Burmese priesthood had been reformed and brought under control; the Government had dealt effectively with the Karen rebellion. The internal dissensions which had weakened the ruling party had been overcome to a large extent. The strengthening of the internal position of Burma and the close and firm friendship which it had established with India were two factors which few people had foreseen. Before 1947, Britain was prone to believe that Burma would continue to be suspicious and hostile towards India and that India, because of the vested interests of the Chettiars and of the settled commercial community, would also be unfriendly towards any nationalist Government of Burma. But the wisdom of the two Prime Ministers and their understanding of the wider issues that both countries had to face have led to a firm understanding between India and Burma which has been a great stabilizing factor in South Asia.

I returned to Peking early in February. Almost immediately after my return Chou En-lai received me. He was greatly interested in the situation in Europe and asked me many questions about the economic and political conditions in England and France. I told him that conditions had greatly improved in England and that the British people were, by and large, moving out of their troubles: that it appeared to me that they had carried out a far-reaching social revolution peacefully and with the least dislocation possible and that any political doctrine which postulated growing social unrest in England would only lead to false conclusions. He was, I thought, greatly surprised at what I told him. The possibility of a peaceful revolution goes against the accepted Marxian doctrine and naturally to one like himself, with very little direct knowledge of non-communist countries, it was unbelievable that a socialist solution provided a working alternative to a communist revolution. Chou En-lai was also very happy about the way the Chinese cultural delegation had been received and welcomed in India and expressed the hope that the Indian goodwill mission would be arriving soon.

At the end of a very long and cordial interview of about two hours, I informed Chou that my Government were ready to discuss the regularization of relations in regard to Tibet. Before I left, Chou had raised this question and had also indicated that he would welcome our good offices for the establishment of direct diplomatic relations with Nepal. I told him that the position in Nepal was a little confused and uncertain and that it would be better to wait for a time before taking up the matter. Chou En-lai promised to discuss the whole thing again with me before long.

At the end of April the Indian goodwill mission arrived in Peking. It was led by Shrimati Vijayalakshmi Pandit and was fairly representative of the cultural life of India. Acharya Narendra Dev and Pandit Amarnath Jha represented academic life and scholarship. There were scientists, economists, engineers, archaeologists—all men of distinction and achievement—on the delegation. Classical Indian dancing was represented by Shanta Rao, while in Bendre the delegation had a painter of repute. I was very well pleased with the composition of the delegation, for I knew that Mrs. Pandit with her great prestige in international life and her charm of manner would create a very good impression on the Chinese, and the rest of the delegation by the variety of their talents would help to bring India home to the Chinese public. The delegation was received with great enthusiasm.

To synchronize with their visit, I had arranged for an exhibition of modern Indian art, which was opened in the Workers' Palace by Chou En-lai. The variety and richness of modern Indian art was a revelation to the Chinese and the exhibition was visited by large crowds every day. In his speech at the time of its opening Chou En-lai alluded to the influence of Indian artistic tradition on China, and instanced the case of the mural paintings in the Tunghuan caves, which he had previously described as a perfect example of Sino-Indian co-operation. Shanta Rao's dances, especially her interpretation of Bharata Natyam and Mohini Attam, were also received with acclamation.

I was happy to be able to utilize Mrs. Pandit's presence to reopen the issue of the Korean peace negotiations. Even before the delegation arrived, I had conveyed to Chou En-lai the suggestion that it might be useful in every way to discuss the question of Korea with Mrs. Pandit, not only because she had been India's

Ambassador in Washington during the entire period of the crisis, but because she would be able to convey personally to Pandit Nehru her own independent appreciation. I therefore arranged for a small intimate dinner at my house. The party consisted only of Chou En-lai, Chang Han-fu, Chen Chia-kang and an interpreter from their side, and Mrs. Pandit, myself, and Kaul from our side. After the dinner we sat apart and discussed at some length the question of the prisoners of war which had become the stumbling-block to the armistice agreement. Chou was insistent that the prisoners on both sides should be repatriated according to normal practice. As the U.S.A. was committed to the opposite point of view I saw no way out of the impasse, but we suggested for the first time the possibility of a neutral examination of the problem. The discussions had one advantage. Mrs. Pandit became firmly convinced that unless some suitable formula to cover this question was evolved the armistice negotiations might finally break down.

Before the delegation left Peking it was received by Mao Tse-tung. Mrs. Pandit had an interesting talk with him and after their conversation he also witnessed Shanta Rao's dance. A Chinese troupe also performed a specially composed dance of welcome to the Indian guests. The climax of that dance was when the stage seemed filled with immense lotus flowers from each of which emerged a woman with the prima ballerina coming out of the central flower. I do not know whether the dance was meant to represent the birth of Lakshmi—a classical theme in Indian mythology—for in that case it was a compliment both to India and to Madame Vijayalakshmi. Chou En-lai told me that the idea of the dance was given by him to the Dance Academy.

After finishing their programme in Peking the delegation went to Manchuria where they had an opportunity of seeing for themselves how far this vital area, which anti-Chinese propaganda had claimed to be under the Soviets, was being run by Kao Kang as the laboratory of socialism. From Manchuria they travelled by special train to the Huai river project, a combined scheme of flood control and irrigation, the first of its kind which New China was undertaking. I also arrived in Shanghai in time to receive them there, for I had arranged for the art exhibition to be opened by Madame Sun Yat-sen at the time of the delegation's visit to the city. Madame Sun Yat-sen was an old friend of the Prime Minister and had been particularly gracious to me ever since my arrival in China in 1948. Even after the revolution we had maintained contact, though, not desiring to embarrass her, I had limited my visits to formal occasions. Her position in New China was something very exceptional. Naturally enough she was a follower of Sun Yat-sen and not a communist. In her house the only portrait on the wall was that of her deceased husband. She lived the life of a lady of culture interested more in good works and devoting herself with single-minded zeal to the great organization which she founded and which had now been taken over by the State—the China Relief Society. Though she was one of the six Vice-Chairmen of the People's Republic she lived generally in Shanghai, supervising her numerous institutions. Only on important public occasions like the 1st of October did she come up to Peking.

Madame Sun Yat-sen received us in her private villa. As the whole delegation was there, she was a little formal and insisted on speaking in Chinese and having herself interpreted. Considering what mastery she has over the English language, Mrs. Pandit thought this rather strange and affected. In fact it was well known that her English was much better than her Mandarin, but the procedure of talking only through interpreters is rigorously followed on formal occasions in China, though in private company the rule is not observed. Madame Sun herself, when she came out to say good-bye, spoke to me privately in English, but the public face had to be maintained.

The next day Madame Sun opened the exhibition and spoke very generously about India. Two days later she attended a dinner which I gave in honour of the delegation which was attended also by Chen Yi and other Party and Government leaders in the city. Since the revolution Madame Sun had never attended a public dinner, and she was good enough to explain to us that while she came to open the exhibition to honour India she came to the dinner in order to show courtesy to me as a friend. Shanta Rao's dance after the dinner was greatly appreciated both by Madame Sun, who had some knowledge of Indian dancing having seen Udai Shankar in Berlin, and by General Chen Yi.

General Chen Yi is in many ways an exceptional man. He appeared to be in his forties, handsome and well set-up, with sparkling eyes and a pleasant manner. His military prowess was legendary, for, between him and Liu Po-cheng, the one-eyed dragon, they had destroyed the military might of Chiang Kai-shek in central China and won the great battle of Suchow. Chen Yi was the military administrator of East China, from Shantung to Fukien, with the civil title of the Mayor of Shanghai. In conversation he appeared to be extremely well informed and discussed intelligently many political problems without the least tinge of dogmatism. But what struck me most about him was his interest in poetry, music, and dancing. He not only understood and appreciated Shanta Rao's dancing and its musical accompaniment, but was able to discuss their finer points. Himself a poet of some repute and a soldier of outstanding achievements, Chen Yi seemed to me to combine the ancient culture of China with the dynamism of the new regime.

Chen Yi also arranged to entertain us with musical and dance performances. A special opera composed by Mei Lan-fang dealing with Buddhist themes was put on for us. The delegation also went to see many of the public institutions of the city and were taken to some factories to see the industrial aspects of New China. From Shanghai they went on to Hanchow and from there to Canton on their return journey. It was a most successful goodwill mission and a great deal of its success was due undoubtedly to the personality and charm of Mrs. Pandit, whose friendliness the Chinese recognized from the very first day of her arrival in Peking.

The Prime Minister had permitted me to relinquish my appointment in Peking after the Mission's return to India. The last month was as usual a round of visits and parties but I was naturally more anxious to secure a settlement of the Tibetan question and to see if anything further could be done about the issue of the prisoners of war in Korea which had become the sole stumbling-block to the armistice negotiations at Panmunjom. Shortly after Mrs. Pandit left I received from the Prime Minister a personal message which contained some proposals which looked promising. Briefly they suggested a neutral commission to take charge of the prisoners with an offer to the northern allies that their representative should have the opportunity of freely interviewing the prisoners and for giving them the necessary explanations. These proposals were understood to have been discussed between Krishna Menon and the authorities in England, though the responsibility for putting them forward remained solely with us. Two days before the date fixed for my departure Chou En-lai invited me to a private dinner at his house and discussed these proposals at length. The impression he gave me was that on principle the proposals were acceptable to the Chinese, though there would have to be close negotiations about the modalities of the control of prisoners during the period of the explanations and the method of interview, etc. His reactions were on the whole satisfactory and I had every reason to feel that the proposals would go through, as they did ultimately, though only after another six months of hard bargaining.

The Tibetan issue was simpler. Chou En-lai recognized the legitimacy of our trade and cultural interests in that area and suggested that the political agency at Lhasa, an office of dubious legality, should be regularized by its transformation into an Indian Consulate-General in exchange for a similar Chinese office in Bombay. This I had been authorized to accept. So far as our other posts and institutions were concerned, some of them like the telegraph lines, military escort at Yatung, were to be abolished quietly in time, and the trade agents and other subordinate agencies brought within the framework of normal consulate relations. These were to be taken up as and when the circumstances became ripe. The main issue of our representation at Lhasa was thus satisfactorily settled and I was happy to feel that there was no outstanding issue between us and the Chinese at the time of my departure.

What was my general impression of New China? I had spent over two years in Peking in close contact with the leaders of the Central People's Government. I had also lived in Nanking when the Kuomintang regime was still powerful and had witnessed its tragic disintegration and final downfall. I had passed a tiresome period of five months, without any recognized official position, but with freedom to observe the growth of a new society. It was a profoundly interesting experience, full of drama, to witness alike the end of an epoch and the beginning of another, the tragic end of the hopes of a great movement, with the inevitable concomitants of national chaos, personal tragedies, sordid betrayals and confusion all round, and the enthusiastic beginning of a new period, hailed as the dawn of a great era, with new ambitions, great hopes and a widespread sense of optimism.

Three impressions of New China stand out clearly in my mind. One is its undoubted aspect as the culminating event of Asian resurgence. In the controversy aroused by the communist character of its revolution, people, more especially in Europe, have been inclined to overlook this basic fact. This resurgence began with the Kuomintang, and in its early and liberal days it represented the great forward movement of Asian peoples in the intermediate period between the two wars. It was not merely the corruption and the political and military weakness of the Kuomintang regime and its utter dependence on America that had deprived "nationalist" China of its position in the vanguard of Asian awakening, but also the fact that it had ceased to represent the new spirit of Asia. The communist leaders, not because of their communism but because they had a greater appreciation of the change that had come over the Asian mind, showed from the beginning a profound realization of the problems of Asia in relation to the West and to America and were therefore more in sympathy with their neighbours.

Secondly, the new Government in China appeared to me the fulfilment of a hundred years of evolution—the movement towards a strong central government which the great mandarins of the later Manchu period had themselves initiated. The Kuomintang had carried the movement forward to some extent; had established a Government whose authority extended over a large area of China. External circumstances, the intervention of Japan, the attitude of the great powers, the alliance of the Chinese capitalist classes who had also come to wield great political authority with the capitalists of the West, and the strength of the local war lords in outlying areas had prevented its consummation. With the establishment of the communist régime, there came into existence in China for the first time in history a strong unified central government having authority over the entire area of the old Celestial Empire, from the borders of Siberia to Indo-China and from the Pacific to the Pamirs. In the old imperial times, under the Hans, the Tangs, the Yuans, the Mings, and the Manchus, no doubt the Empire had been united under a central authority, but the character of that authority, dependent on the mystique of a Son of Heaven with a divine mandate exercising his control through great viceroys, was different from the all-pervasiveness of the Central People's Government with the whole paraphernalia of rail and air communications, telegraph and wireless and, above all, a powerful national army and an indoctrinated and disciplined party spread all over the country. This central-ization may or may not be a good thing, but it is a fact of supreme importance as it has converted what was an inchoate mass into a united nation, capable of organizing and bringing into use the immense resources of China. By this process China had become in fact, what it had always claimed to be, a Great Power.

Abbot, in his *Expansion of Europe* says: "Among the many diverse events which make a period memorable in history none is more striking than the rise of a State to equality or supremacy among the powers of the world. Preceded almost invariably by a long period of slow development, precipitated by the advent of some extraordinary circumstance, or the ambition or ability of some individual, and culminating for the most part in a great convulsion, a final arbitrament of arms, with its vast expenditure of energy, treasure, and blood, and the relative decline and re-adjustment of other powers of the polity into which the new power thrusts its way, this recurrent phenomenon of history is at once the chief motive of progress and distinction in the drama of politics." This phenomenon was in fact what we were witnessing in the Far East. China had become a Great Power and was insisting on being recognized as such. The adjustments which such a recogni-tion requires are not easy, and the conflict in the Far East is the

M

outcome of this contradiction. This could be seen in every aspect of the life of New China, in its assertiveness, in its belligerence, in its defiance of those who deny her rights, no less than in the enthusiasm of the people, in the great release of energy which can be seen everywhere, in the determination to catch up with other nations, not only in power, but in industrial and other greatness. It is in fact one of the main motive forces of whatever is good and bad in New China.

The third characteristic which impressed me was China's desire to maintain the continuity of her life and culture, while destroying ruthlessly what the leaders of new thought described as feudal and reactionary excrescence. The Chinese have shown no desire to be anything other than Chinese. Their admiration of the achievements of the Soviet Union has not led them either to give up their clothes, their food, their courtesies, or their ways of life. Determined enemies of Confucianism, with its five obediences and its rituals, its canonical texts, and its artificial ways of writing and speaking, the leaders of New China have been able to relate their present to their past by a re-interpretation of their history. The veneration and care with which they preserve their ancient monuments, the new life they have given to old forms of artistic expression, the enthusiasm for research into the earlier periods of Chinese history—all these are evidences of the same spirit.

The desire for education, for rapid advancement in all fields, a determination to quicken the tempo of things generally, were evident everywhere. No doubt the driving force came from the communist party, but large sections of people seemed to me to have been infected by this enthusiasm. They showed little tolerance for those who hung back, and were ruthless with people who opposed all this activity. That strange phenomenon the "San Fan" movement, which was organized as a great national struggle against "bureaucratism," complacency and general sliding back, was but one aspect of this determined drive towards advancement. Among the cadres even of the communist party, in the universities, among business circles, from top to bottom there was, for a period of six months, a vigorous campaign organized on a national scale which involved public accusations, confessions, and strange procedures amounting to what appeared to me as psychological torture, the sole object of which was to ensure purity in public conduct and greater efficiency in work. The objects were no doubt excellent but the means somehow made me think of the Inquisition and other earlier attempts to purify the human mind by force.

In general I may summarize my impression of New China as a tremendous upheaval which has transformed what was a highly civilized but unorganized mass of people into a great modern State. It has released great energies, given the Chinese people a new hope, and a new vision of things. It has brought forth great enthusiasm and an irresistible desire to move forward, but the means employed to achieve these very desirable ends are in many cases of a kind which revolts the free mind. Compared to the State the individual has lost all value and this is the strange thing in China which adds a tinge of sorrow even when one appreciates and admires what the revolution has done for China and Asia generally.

INDEX